Midnight Sun, Arctic Moon

Midnight Sun, Arctic Moon

MAPPING THE WILD HEART OF ALASKA

⌒

MARY ALBANESE

EPICENTER PRESS

Epicenter is a regional press publishing nonfiction books about the arts, history, environment, and diverse cultures and lifestyles of Alaska and the Pacific Northwest.

Publisher: Kent Sturgis
Acquisitions Editor: Lael Morgan
Manuscript Editor: Kent Sturgis
Proofreader: Melanie Wells
Indexer: Sherrill Carlson
Cover & text design: Betty Watson, Watson Design
Mapmaker: Marge Mueller, Gray Mouse Graphics
Printer: McNaughton & Gunn

Photos ©2012, Mary Albanese family photos unless otherwise credited.

Photo credits: *Front cover:* Image is a digital combination of a photo of a helicopter waiting to retrieve the author from a ridgeline near McGrath, Alaska, and a photo of the author carrying a full field pack; *Back cover:* the author's camp on Sugar Loaf Mountain overlooking Mount McKinley *Text:* page 100, top photo, Steve Clautice; page 108, wedding photo by Ron Brooks; photo of author by Ralph Jordan; page 175, photo of Tom Albanese by Mark Zdepski; page 179, bottom photo courtesy of DGGS; page 181, large photo by S. Merchetti; page 184, lower photo by Russ White; page 215, author photo by Amy Albanese.

Library of Congress Control Number: 2011946201
ISBN 978-1-935347-17-0

10 9 8 7 6 5 4 3 2 1
Printed in the United States of America

To order single copies of MIDNIGHT SUN, ARCTIC MOON, mail $14.95 plus $6 for shipping (WA residents add $1.90 state sales tax) to Epicenter Press, PO Box 82368, Kenmore, WA 98028; call us day or night at 800-950-6663, or visit www.EpicenterPress.com.

Like *Epicenter Press Alaska Book Adventures* on ◼ Facebook

For all my families—
the one I was born to that
encouraged my dreams,
the one that Tom and I made, and
the ones that so generously took me in,
including my New Jersey crew,
my film folks,
the talented botanical artists,
my amazing sisterhood
(with one brother) of writers,
and my dear Alaska family
that has meant so much.

Contents

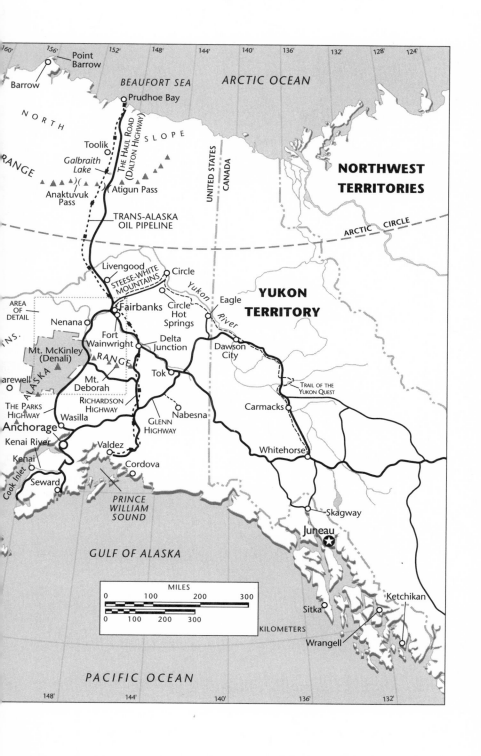

Foreword

$\mathcal{I}$T ISN'T JUST THE FACT THAT MARY ALBANESE survived in a male-dominated field—geology. Or that she did so in a punishing country—Alaska's arctic and sub-arctic. Or that her exploration of uncharted geothermal resources, ancient volcanic debris, and previously unknown mineral deposits took her beyond the edge of existing maps, requiring her to draw her own.

What really makes *Midnight Sun, Arctic Moon* fascinating is that it is an amusing, no-holds-barred, coming-of-age story of the kind women seldom write. It offers a rare look at the aspirations of a bizarrely remote young state, of its mainstay university, and of a remarkable young woman irresistibly drawn to the Far North—all driven early in the Age of Aquarius by their own dawning.

Although raised conventionally in Cicero, New York, Albanese inherited the itchy foot that had alternately plagued and delighted her forebears, causing her to set her sights on Alaska for no reasons she can identify. By all odds she should have become a school teacher. How the well-qualified and personable twenty-three-year-old redhead managed to get turned down for teaching jobs by dozens of schools in the Far North remains a puzzle. Stranger yet, she actually stumbled into geology, yet pursued it as aggressively as if it were a life-long dream.

Never mind that this field requires unusual brawn and endurance. Or that Albanese stood just five foot five, and weighed less than the two suitcases and one carry-on filled with all her worldly possessions that she squeezed onto the flight to Alaska. Or that her penchant for science was challenged by her love of the arts. Driven by a low threshold of boredom, curiosity with many dimensions, and a sense of humor that wouldn't quit, Albanese charted an uneven but daring course to womanhood with startling results.

The region that she set out to map with diversified teams of scientists turned out to be a war zone fraught with marauding bears, plane wrecks, and more than the usual human traumas spawned by hardship, depravation, and isolation. Yet Albanese made lasting friendships and a unique marriage, while acquiring the self-assurance that comes with a job well done and a strong winning streak. Even a crushing personal tragedy did not impede her resolve or dampen her spirit, although her love affair with Alaska became increasingly complicated.

You don't need to know or care about geology to become engrossed in Mary Albanese's story. It's a compelling history of an exciting but little reported era, and a darned good read.

Lael Morgan

Preface

My PACK, HEAVY WITH ROCKS, dug into my back as I hiked across the uneven ground twenty miles (32 kilometers) from the Arctic Circle. There was no trail here—no roads, no buildings, and no people for miles. The rocks here had never been mapped. That was my job. I was a geologist on foot, and that's why I found myself in this northern wilderness with nothing but scrub brush, shivering pine, and the rocks—always the rocks.

I had been hiking for hours, checking every outcrop, measuring angles, and breaking off chunks of stone with my hammer.

The sun was high in the summer sky. Instead of setting that night, the sun would blanket the land in a cool orange glow. At noon, though, the sun was bright and strong.

I was hot. I had been slogging across the tundra for six hours, and my forehead was drenched with sweat.

My skull felt like hell-fire. I knew this was a warning. As one of few women in a field dominated by men, I didn't tell anyone about my tendency to pass out from heat stroke. I was dangerously close to having one now. I needed to cool down.

I didn't have time to rest. I had too many miles to go to make my target. As a girl not long out of my teens, I didn't have the strength or speed of the men on the crew, so I had to work harder to do the same job. I wasn't going to allow anything to stop me from covering as much ground as anyone else.

I studied the contour map. If I veered to the right, I should run into a creek about a half-mile ahead. I figured I could get there before I passed out.

The creek was where I thought it would be. It wasn't anything to brag about, just a trickle of water, but its edges were lined with a snow-frosted crust. Perfect.

I took off my hat, a cotton baseball cap, and packed it with snow. When I put it back on, the crown of my head was encased in a bowl of ice. The relief was immediate. I could go for another hour at least. By the time the snow had melted and run down my shirt, the sun would be lower and cooler. Heat stroke averted, I set off again.

Suddenly, I heard something in the trees behind me crashing and thrashing. It sounded big, but when I looked back, I didn't see anything. It was probably a moose. I kept going.

Then I heard it again. It was following me. Moose didn't behave that way. It was less than a hundred feet away (30 m) when it emerged from behind a tree—a black bear lumbering towards me.

The bear's head looked small. This wasn't good. In the tundra, it is hard to judge size from a distance. With a bear, the rule of thumb is *small head means big body*. This bear had a pinhead, telling me that its body had to be huge—a fully grown adult. I couldn't out-run it, couldn't out-climb it. I was no match at all.

Without stopping, I pulled out my radio, a black state-of-the-art walkie-talkie the size of a quart bottle of milk and just as heavy. It was the best equipment there was, able to transmit several miles in a straight line. Unfortunately, out here in the mountains and gullies, not much was straight.

"This is Mary," I spoke into the walkie-talkie. "Mike, are you there?"

"Chopper Mike," as we called our helicopter pilot, would be parked in these hills somewhere. Calm and steady, he listened to his radio for any signs of trouble. But with five of us out in the field, working as far as ten miles apart, Mike could be fifty miles (84 km) away.

No reply. Chopper Mike was out of range.

"Can anyone hear me?" I said, hoping to relay the message.

Still no answer.

"This is Mary," I said. "If anyone gets this, tell Mike I need a pickup. Now!"

I shoved the radio back into my pack and went on, moving as fast as I dared, willing myself not to sweat. I had heard that bears can smell fear, and had spent enough time with animals on the farm to believe this was most likely true. If I could convince this bear that I wasn't afraid, maybe it would wander off.

No such luck. It kept coming, closer every moment.

This was a black bear, smaller than a grizzly, but capable of tearing a person apart. I could see this one was looking for trouble. I would have to face it.

Not long before, another field geologist had come across a black bear like this. She was unarmed because her boss didn't believe in guns. So when the bear came at her, she had no defense. She decided to play dead, having heard that if you played dead, the bear might lose interest. This probably saved her life. Still, before he lost interest, the bear tossed her around like a rag doll, ripping her arms out of their sockets.

That wasn't going to happen to me. I pulled out the new blue-steel .44 Magnum pistol I had gotten for my birthday—not a gift I would have been given if I stayed in New York state to teach science in a comfortable high school. I had abandoned that goal long ago, although it looked mighty attractive right now. How had I ended up here staring down a stubby four-inch gun barrel at an oncoming bear?

My Magnum was the biggest pistol made. Still, it was just a handgun, reminding me of the endless debates I had heard in the bars back in Fairbanks: Would a pistol, *any* pistol, have sufficient firepower to drop a charging bear?

As I steadied my aim, it looked as if I was about to find out.

1.

❧ Big Dreams ❧

I WAS BORN IN THE SNOW BELT of upstate New York in 1954, not far from the Canadian border, on a few acres we called Buttercup Farm. I was the tomboy sister, the second of three girls with a brother on the end. As a child, I was lulled to sleep by stories of our family told by my grandfather, who had a way of making the adventures from the past come alive.

In the 1800s, when travel was difficult and people rarely left home, my great-grandfather had been a sailor traveling the world to far-flung ports before settling near the shores of Oneida Lake in New York state. Before him, my great-great-grandfather had explored the Wild West after serving as General George Custer's personal bodyguard during the Civil War.

Three wars later, my father traveled to remote Pacific islands on a construction mission, repairing the damage of World War II before settling down in his farmhouse north of Syracuse. He dreamed of "retiring" to the West Coast and exploring the small towns of the region as an itinerant carpenter. Raised in a family of world travelers and adventurers, it is no wonder that as I grew, my dreams grew too, until they became too big to fit into the confines of our sleepy little town of Cicero, New York.

At seventeen, armed with a New York State Regents Scholarship, I went off to college in the most exotic corner of the state I could find— Long Island. There I found an international flavor and an exhilarating cultural diversity mixed with the sophistication of nearby New York City. Yet, watching my heavily perfumed roommates totter to their classes in spiked heels, I felt like a tourist. I would never belong here. There was somewhere else for me, though I didn't know then where that somewhere was.

Meanwhile, I studied earth science, discovering the planet's secrets with the wonder of an explorer, amazed by the way each layer was built upon the one before in a giant puzzle of rock. The second year, I added a program in environmental studies. Studying two programs at once was a lot of work, but it allowed me not only to see how the world was put together, but also how it might change in the future.

At the same time, I took classes in drawing and painting. Art was like meditation for me. It relaxed my mind and alleviated the stress of pursuing two science degrees. I accumulated so many art credits that I qualified for a fine-arts degree as well, delighted by the prospect of earning three degrees for the price of one.

I didn't mind the long hours. But what concerned me was being unable to commit to one field. Was I wasting my time going in so many directions? Was there some job that could benefit from all three fields of study?

I knew I could teach. As a teacher, a diverse background would be handy, especially if I taught in a small, rural school where I might be asked to handle more than one subject. I had an aptitude for teaching, having tutored kids with reading problems back in high school. As I looked to my future, teaching seemed like an excellent path. And by shifting from science-research to science-teaching, I cut out some of the most difficult math and science courses. This made my multiple programs more manageable.

As I polished off my courses, an idea came to me to go north to Alaska. I don't recall where it came from, or when it changed from an idea into an obsession. All I know is that it grew until I couldn't ignore it, until I felt that if I didn't go there I would miss something important and my life would never feel complete.

In 1977, when I graduated with three degrees and a teaching certification in science, news reports told of a severe shortage of teachers in Alaska, especially in science and math. The press called it a crisis. I had already taught high-school biology, earth science, and astronomy as a student teacher. I had written and conducted educational shows for planetariums, spent a summer teaching math to young adult offenders in prison, and taught art at a mental hospital. Fresh out of college, I already had assembled a varied portfolio of teaching experience. They could throw me into any classroom, assign any subject, and I knew I would thrive. I was exactly the sort of teacher Alaska needed. With my desire to go north, and Alaska's demand for educators, the pieces of my career seemed to be coming together.

That summer I sent out applications to every school district in Alaska. I generated a staggering pile of paperwork, leaving nothing to chance. From the big modern schools in Anchorage to the one-room school houses in the remote villages, they all heard from me. But few responded, and those responses were polite, apologetic rejections. A few school officials explained that they had offered jobs to candidates from New York in the past, but that those teachers failed to arrive. Apparently, New Yorkers had a reputation for making very bad Alaskans. Although the newspapers continued to bemoan Alaska's teacher shortage, there was nothing for me—no job offer, no interview, no wait-list, not even a friendly "maybe."

Still, my dream called and wouldn't let me give up. I had to find another way.

2.

~ *North* ~

$\mathcal{W}$ITH A TEACHING JOB OFF THE TABLE, I took stock. What else could I do? What did I know well enough to get me to the far north?

The answer was right there in my transcripts, in that impossibly long list of courses I had taken and degrees earned. *I was good at studying.* I understood academic life and knew how to get a student loan. I was already in debt up to my ears. Another year of borrowing would be a drop in the bucket.

I learned that Alaska had a fine university system with graduate programs at the campus in Fairbanks. If I studied there for a year, I would become a resident. Then it would be hard for the schools to turn me away.

Even better, the Education Department on the Fairbanks campus offered a tidy one-year master's degree program in teaching. With that under my belt, I could enter the job market at a higher pay grade. How exciting to find a program that could pay for itself in a short time. I sent off an application.

The Fairbanks campus also offered a master's degree in geology. With my degree in science-teaching, I wasn't particularly qualified for an advanced geology-research program but it didn't hurt to apply. All they could do was reject me, hardly a novel experience after my dismal job search.

By late July, my student loan was approved, and I was accepted into the University of Alaska as a graduate student in the Education Department. A week later, I received another letter, this one from the Geology Department. To my surprise, the Geology Department accepted me into its graduate program as well. Now, I not only had a way to get there, I had a choice.

I wrote to both departments, explaining the situation. They understood and invited me to come to the campus and decide once I got there. I was closing in on my dream. I spent every last penny I had on the airfare and started to pack.

My family was proud that I had found a way to follow my heart. Although Alaska was on the other side of the planet, my goals made sense, considerably more so than my older sister Christine's career path. She had dropped out of college to join a carnival that promised her the chance to see the world. The troupe toured the Deep South, where Christine learned to run games like the ball toss, the spin-to-win, and the rat race where carnival-goers bet on live rats. After six months, she realized that this lifestyle was not very glamorous after all and returned to New York, where she eventually earned a teaching degree.

My father was almost as excited about Alaska as I was. He had not yet achieved his dream of moving out west. With my younger sister Stephanie and brother Ed still in school, my father had a few more years to go before he could retire. In the meantime, he could enjoy my adventures vicariously.

I counted down the days until my departure, each hour a torturous wait as I tried to keep a lid on my expectations. I had such grand hopes for a place I had never seen. Would the real Alaska, or any other place on earth, live up to my fantasy?

As the long days of summer drew to a close, it was time to find out.

My entire family piled into the station wagon to see me off on August 20, 1977. I had a one-way ticket; if things didn't work out, I wouldn't have enough money to get back.

My brother Ed wore a yellow tee-shirt to the airport. It was so bright that as my plane taxied down the runway, I could still see him pressed up against the glass in the terminal, my last glimpse of home.

The Pan American flight to Fairbanks was full. Back then, smoking was allowed on flights. With more than seven hundred passengers, many of them smokers, the air soon turned from stale to vile to toxic as the hours passed. I tried to take very short breaths.

On the other side of the aisle was a couple that had met in Fairbanks during their college years and were heading north again for a forty-year reunion. Despite their love of Alaska, they had moved south, after graduating, to Ohio where the husband worked as an engineer.

Their eyes glistened as they spoke of their Alaska days. With such strong feelings, I wondered how they could have left.

Then darkness settled, and the plane grew quiet as people dozed off. Not me. I was too excited to sleep, convinced that something amazing might happen.

Five hours into the flight, an eerie orange stain appeared outside my window, like an egg yolk smattered across the horizon. Behind us the sky was pure black, but ahead, that splash of color was my first glimpse of the arctic sun. It oozed across the horizon for an hour before the sun finally retreated—not in a blaze of glory as it does elsewhere, but languidly, seductively.

It was dark again when we landed at Fairbanks International Airport shortly before midnight. The stewardess cranked open the airplane's heavy door, and my first sense of Alaska was the cool night air that rushed in fragranced with the tang of tar pine. The Alaska night sky was an endless swath of velvet sapphire gray, punctured by forest spires pointing up to a waxing moon that threw long shadows onto the tarmac. As I took my first steps onto Alaska soil, I was caught in a shaft of pale green light as the moon punched a hole in the cool darkness above and smiled down on me.

<hr />

The night bus wove through the campus passing buildings perched on a hill overlooking the Tanana Valley. I wasn't expecting igloos, but I was surprised how modern the campus looked with steel and concrete buildings and a modern cafeteria and commons featuring an entire wall made from panels of glass.

I lugged my bags across campus to Nerland Hall, the dormitory that housed the graduate students. Nicknamed "Nerd Land Hall," it really did feel like the land of the nerds with so many grad students living under one roof. I felt right at home.

My room was a ten-by-ten square with two beds, two desks, and a roommate who was pleasant enough if you had to have a roommate.

By then it was the middle of the night. After a brief introduction, I slid my bags under the desk, crawled into my bed, and fell asleep. For the first time in years, I didn't have to dream of being in Alaska, I was there.

3.

~ *Finding My Way* ~

THE SUNLIGHT POURED IN at an obscenely early hour, preventing any more sleep. I jumped up and ran to the window expecting a magnificent view, but all I could see were the concrete walkways between the institutional structures. Beyond that was a hazy blur.

Summer was the forest-fire season. It had been a dry summer, and the Tanana Flats were burning, choking the southern sky with smoke. A strange low cloud shaped like a series of lumps clung to the horizon. It didn't move for two days.

On the third morning, the smoky haze lifted. The lumps were still there on the horizon, but they weren't clouds. They were snow-capped mountain peaks of the Alaska Range. I came to learn their names—Mount Deborah, Mount Hess, and Mount Hayes. A fourth peak to the west was the mightiest mountain of them all, Denali, "the Great One," as the Indians called it. Also known as Mount McKinley, it stood 20,320 feet (6,193 m), the highest point in North America. I could see blue shadows caressing its snow line, clear and sharp, even though it was one hundred fifty miles (240 km) away.

It wasn't long before I learned that this mountain had a secret. As seen from Fairbanks just right before sunset, Denali sometimes grew to three times its size, towering over everything else on the horizon. It was an arctic mirage caused by a refraction of light. The first time I saw it, I thought my imagination had run away with my mind. I was relieved that others saw it, too. After that, I felt sorry for all the places in the world that didn't have a mountain that rose up like Shangri La and shrank back down the next morning. On those evenings when its magnification was extreme, I would hear people on the streets saying, "Did you see the mountain?" No one had to ask which mountain. We all knew it was Denali, the Great One, of course.

On every car was a reminder of the magic of this place. The license plates read, "Alaska, the Last Frontier." It certainly was. Few roads led out of Fairbanks connecting to anywhere else, and on a dark night you could drive into the hills flanking the town and see far out to the horizon. In the view that stretched in every direction, there were few pinpoints of light punctuating the velvet shades of night, a visual reminder of how alone our town stood in the wilds of the interior basin. The sense of isolation was palpable but invigorating. People up here had no room for self-pity—only self-reliance. We had that in abundance.

As for Fairbanks, it wasn't much of a town. The downtown housed a string of bars, a few pawnshops, and some raunchy hotels among overpriced tourist shops. Construction of the trans-Alaska oil pipeline had been completed two months before, having attracted thousands of workers who came up from the Lower 48 states to make a quick buck. The bars had been more than happy to relieve the workers of their paychecks, and saloon brawls and domestic violence were common. The pawn shops would sell you a gun over the counter, no questions asked. In this explosive mix, a night on the town offered a different wild life experience than that promised in the tour brochures.

Five miles (8 km) from town at the other end of the spectrum was the main campus of the University of Alaska, the crown jewel of Fairbanks, the northernmost university in the world.

The campus was laid out in a logical pattern. Off to one side was the Beluga, a giant white inflated building that looked like the top of a monstrous whale. This oversized balloon held a sports complex including a track where you could run laps year-round to keep fit. But you couldn't have a conversation in there. To keep it inflated, the building was continuously pumped with hot air. The constant whoosh of air was deafening.

The other buildings on campus were more conventional, having windows and solid walls and roofs. To the northwest, beyond a long ledge of rock, was the West Ridge with its imposing compound of research buildings. Here scientists conducted studies of the unique conditions of the north, including the arctic migrations, glacial research, and the aurora borealis, or northern lights.

The dormitories were grouped near the center of campus. One dorm, Wickersham Hall, housed women only. Students who lived there were called Wick-chicks. The first Wick-chick I met was a sprightly seventy-year-old woman who enjoyed meeting new people, learning new things, and eating meals she didn't have to cook. As she said about her life as a perpetual student, "What's not to like?" But overwhelmingly, the students were men, outnumbering the women in Fairbanks by a healthy margin. As the tee-shirts said about Alaska men, "The odds are good, but the goods are odd." I couldn't disagree with that as I watched the young men scurrying across campus, most with more hair on their chins than on top of their heads.

You had to be pretty eccentric to stand out, but some did. Those first few days I met a Hell's Angels biker dude with fingernails over an inch long, and twin brothers who rappelled down the cliff at the edge of campus wearing climbing boots, a rope harness, and nothing else. That made the six o'clock news.

In the middle of the campus, next to a fenced patch of grass, was a garden with vegetables that grew freakishly large under the midnight sun, including cabbages the size of a dishwasher. Apparently in the all-night sunshine, their growth hormones didn't know when to stop.

It was in this surreal setting that I considered my options. To plan for the fall term, I needed to choose between two paths that would take my life in sharply different directions.

It made sense for me to enroll in the Education Department's one-year Master of Arts in teaching program. Teaching was where I was headed, and this would help me get there. The other choice, becoming a research geologist, was a bit out of my league. But the Geology Department had accepted me, too, so I thought I should stop by in person to decline its offer.

I found the Geology Department office on the top floor of the Brooks Building, a five-story concrete block with windows perpetually stained from decades of rock dust and sulfur from the basement labs. Built in the 1920s, with its multi-story structure and electric lights *in every room* it had once been a marvel of arctic architecture. By the late 1970s, it was a tired old relic coated with grit.

The chairman of the Geology Department, Dr. David Stone, had an office on the top floor. I walked up the five flights of stairs (no elevators here) but Dr. Stone wasn't in. As I headed back down, I met Dr. Mickey Payne, the new petroleum geology professor with a smooth

Texas drawl. To get to know the students, he was organizing a field trip to the Brooks Range. He invited me to come for an introduction to the geology of the state.

I had no idea where the Brooks Range was, but I took an information sheet and told him I would let him know.

Then I made my way across campus to the Education Department located in a gleaming modern high rise with bright airy windows, commanding views from the upper floors, and elevators to get you there. It was so much more impressive than the old Brooks Building. I introduced myself to the department chairman, a tall man with a beard, and we talked about teaching in the bush. He had been a rural school teacher before joining the university. Now as the head of the department, he had one of the most important educational positions in the state. I could foresee my own teaching career—working in a small rural school, then another, getting to know different parts of the state. I would fit in well here.

As the conversation wound down, he asked if I had been anywhere interesting so far. I told him I had just arrived but was thinking about going to the Brooks Range.

That stopped him cold. The Brooks Range? How would I go there? It was Alaska's farthest-north mountain range, well north of the Arctic Circle and several hundred miles away. One of the most remote mountain ranges in the world, the Brooks Range stretched across the state from the Canadian border to the Bering Sea. The only way to drive there was on a gravel road, closed to the public, which serviced the trans-Alaska pipeline.

I checked my flyer to see if I had made a mistake. I hadn't.

The man sighed. Perhaps, he said, he would get a chance to see those arctic mountains for himself some day.

That moment changed my life. All of a sudden, joining the Education Department seemed like a dim second choice. I could work as a teacher for years, like this professor before me, and never have the opportunities of a geology student stumbling into the Brooks Building for the first time.

In an instant, my mind was made up. I had to go see those arctic mountains. I knew my geology background wasn't strong enough for research, but the Geology Department had accepted me into their master's program anyway. This was the direction I would take. It was time to go back and tell them the good news.

I retraced my steps back to the Brooks Building and found Dr. Stone in his office. The Geology Department chairman had a fine British accent and a passion for geophysics that radiated from him like a humming microwave tower. I later heard that during the big earthquake of 1964, when everyone else was running for cover, Dr. Stone was seen running down College Road chasing the ground waves, leaping from crest to crest as the road's surface rose and fell. Facing this human dynamo of the geophysical world, I made my announcement: I was going to be a geologist!

Dr. Stone went quiet for a moment and his face went pale. Then he cleared his throat and explained that I would need to make up a lot of undergraduate course work first, and not just in geology. I would have to take more calculus and chemistry to meet the entry requirements.

This was a lot to take on and part of me wondered if I could handle it. I had barely passed calculus. What made me think I would survive the advanced version?

Still, those mountains were so tempting. The state's geological maps were filled with huge unexplained gaps, and here was a chance to do something big—to stamp my initials on some of those maps. Whatever the cost, could I really let this opportunity slip through my fingers?

Okay, I told Dr. Stone. Sign me up—whatever it takes.

I did not know until years later why the chairman had seemed shocked. Apparently my acceptance into the program had been a mistake. The staff had misplaced my files, twice, and was too embarrassed to ask for my transcripts a third time. It was assumed that I had fulfilled the minimum requirements. When the transcripts resurfaced, Dr. Stone realized how under-qualified I was and didn't believe I would show up ready to pitch in. To be honest, I wouldn't have laid odds on it myself.

Together, we outlined all the extra classes I would have to take, including a six-week field camp course the following summer. This provided intensive training and mapping designed to give students actual field experience. After all of these classes I would begin graduate-level courses and complete a thesis.

Sitting there in his office, hearing all of this compressed into a few sentences, I didn't think it sounded too bad. Wasn't a thesis just an extra-long essay? In my blissful ignorance, I had no idea what I was getting myself into, or how formidable this thesis would be.

Frankly, Dr. Stone doubted I could do it. It was a tall order, with more qualified students dropping out all the time. But he gave me the chance. Whatever I did with it would be up to me.

4.

⊱ Sky over Toolik ⊰

ON THE DAY OF THE BROOKS RANGE field trip, I woke up early, eager to be off. My duffel bag was packed with clothes for three days along with two blankets, my make-shift substitute for a sleeping bag. I set off to meet the group, having been told they would be waiting at the parking lot at the "bottom of the hill."

I went to the small parking lot behind the Brooks Building, but it was deserted. I climbed the little hill and noticed another parking lot, and another, and yet another, all next to various hills. All were empty. At this early hour on a weekend, the campus was like a ghost town.

The campus stretched for almost a mile, with buildings in every direction, each with its own parking lot, each with a hill. From the grassy knolls to the steep cliffs, I had no idea where to go.

I dragged my bag from one parking lot to another, trying to ignore my watch as the minutes ticked by. Now I was no longer early; I was exactly on time, but lost. If I didn't find them soon, the group would leave without me, and I would miss the trip that had shifted my future.

I climbed the most massive hill, up a dozen flights of stairs bolted into the side of a cliff. From here I could see even more buildings but no people, no cars, and no staging area for an expedition to the arctic. I sat down on the curb of the road that threaded through campus, exhausted, angry at myself, and frustrated beyond belief. My insides heaved and my breakfast threatened to come up. Not that it would have mattered; there was no one to notice.

Then a red pickup truck puttered up and stopped.

"You're not looking for the Brooks Range trip, are you?" asked a man with white hair, a salt and pepper beard, and piercing hazel eyes. It was the sedimentology professor, kindly trolling for lost souls.

"Yes, I am!" I said, hardly able to believe my luck.

"Hop in," he said. "I'm Dr. Don Triplehorn, but you can call me Tripp. Everybody does."

I threw my bag into the back and climbed in. Five minutes later, Dr. Tripp pulled the truck onto a gravel pad, hidden by a hill, buzzing with activity. People stacked boxes of food into a haphazard convoy of vehicles. Some were loaded with gear, some carried people, and one carried fuel drums, a hand pump, and a stack of spare tires. It looked like a traveling service station, and it was. What was then called the Haul Road (later renamed the Dalton Highway) was a 415-mile (667 km) dirt road from Fairbanks to the Arctic Coast. Nearly twice the distance from London to Paris, this road didn't have a single store, rest stop, or even a fuel station. You had to bring everything with you.

The students were bunched up in three vans. Wafting out of the first van were peals of good-natured laughter. This sounded like a fun group. I couldn't ask for a better setting to meet my fellow students. Unfortunately, that van was already full.

In the second truck, the people were not quite as boisterous, but they seemed friendly. There was no more room here, either. I headed over to the third van. I found eight people sitting inside, but no one spoke. I said hello and received cold stares and suspicious grunts as I squeezed my way into the last seat in the back row. The drive was going to be a long one but at least I wasn't left behind.

On our way out of town, we stopped at the last commercial establishment we would see for three days, a combination store and saloon made of plywood, planks, and logs looking like a set for an old John Wayne western. Our driver went inside for some gum. While we waited in the van, a woman with dark hair stumbled out of the saloon and fell down in the dirt. The people with me looked the other way.

I wanted to help her to her feet but I was stuck in the back and couldn't get out.

"Shouldn't we help her?" I asked.

Silence.

A student named Rita in the front seat glanced back at me and then looked away. She was a graduate student two years ahead of me with her field research already finished. I was impressed by her field experience, but not by what she said next.

"You can always tell a new one," she muttered. "Never saw a drunken native before."

I was new, perhaps annoyingly new, but with that attitude, I knew it was Rita who didn't belong here.

North of Fairbanks, after the paved road had turned to gravel, we found ourselves at a barbed-wire gate with the Haul Road stretching beyond. A guard approached, a gun swinging at his hip. He doubled-checked our paperwork, then waved us through.

We stopped next to the pipeline, a tube of metal running down the middle of Alaska, eight hundred miles (1,280 km) from the Prudhoe Bay oilfields to Valdez, an ice-free port on Prince William Sound. It had taken two years to build and was completed on June 20, 1977, two months earlier. In photos, the pipeline is dwarfed by the vast wilderness, and the pipe looks like a thin steel snake zig-zagging across the tundra. Standing beside it, the forty-eight-inch pipe loomed above us on vertical beams cradled by massive springs designed to flex in an earthquake.

The support beams were refrigerated so that the oil, steaming hot when it came from the ground, wouldn't melt the permafrost, the perpetually frozen soil found in about eighty percent of Alaska. In other words, for three out of every four steps you take in Alaska, you are likely to be walking on frozen ground. Even in the summer, the cold is never far away.

Cramming ourselves back into the vans, we headed north with no other vehicles in sight. About twenty minutes into the trip, it began to get dark. This made no sense; it was too early for dusk. Then I realized the sun wasn't going down. Instead, my glasses were becoming coated with a thick growing layer of sepia dust, kicked up from the dirt road. Even with the windows rolled up, that dust penetrated everywhere—on our clothes, on our skin, and I wondered about my lungs. For the next three days, I had to wipe down my glasses every twenty minutes in order to see.

We stopped along the way to inspect different rock formations. I welcomed the chance to stretch my legs, breathe the fresh air, and learn about the rocks.

At our third stop, a series of explosions suddenly erupted near my feet. It sounded like gunshots and instinctively I ducked. But it was only firecrackers set off by Dr. John Dillon, the world's leading expert on the Brooks Range. As a state geologist, he had mapped more of this remote region than anyone else.

"I just wanted to make sure you're all awake," he said with a grin that emerged from his heavy black beard. Then he told us about the rock face before us, his arms waving, his face flushed with excitement as he spoke of the formations as if they were old friends. In a way, they were. I realized that while these rocks were unique, so were the characters who studied them.

Continuing north, we came to a sign next to a scrubby swamp that read: "Welcome to the Arctic Circle." This entryway to the arctic was hardly impressive, and it didn't take long to see that arctic swamps are as foul as stagnant mud patches anywhere. The only difference is that in the arctic, the bugs are more desperate. We were peppered with greedy no-see-ums and mosquitoes that wanted our blood.

Later, we stopped at Franklin Bluffs, a desolate stretch of country with fierce winds that chased us back into the vans. We had to skip that lecture. No one could hear the professor over the wind. Back inside the van, our driver explained that the bluffs were named after an explorer who had died of exposure not far from here. One of the students thought this was funny.

"Franklin Bluffs!" he said. "What a place, so pathetic that the only thing that ever happened here was that somebody died. What should we call it? Let's name it after the dead guy!"

I didn't share his amusement, but I understood the point. Explorers losing battles with the elements were events from the distant past. I tried in vain to picture this brave explorer who had given his life charting the land. I wouldn't have believed that within a year, my brash young colleague would face his own mortality in an equally remote part of the arctic, or that his fate would rest on one person—me.

~

Further north, the straggly spruce trees got smaller and smaller until they didn't grow higher than three feet tall. Then even these miniature trees dwindled away until there were none. We were north of the tree-line; from here on, it was too cold for any kind of tree to grow.

Meanwhile, the mountains buckled up, then reared overhead,

flanking us on either side. The road scraped the bottom of a broad
bowl-shaped valley between the peaks as we wound through
Anaktuvuk Pass, our convoy clinging to the winding gravel road
between jagged mountain spires that grazed the clouds. I had been
to the Alps once, but had never seen anything like this Tolkien-like
landscape. But this was not Middle Earth; it was North Earth, an actual
place.

We parked the vans to hike around. As I clambered up a slope, I
found a fossil pressed into a piece of rock. It was a brachiopod, a clam-
like creature that had gone extinct eons ago. This fossilized shell told
the story of an inland sea that had once covered this ground. I showed
it to a third-year grad student who specialized in fossils.

"Where did you find this?" he asked. "No one has ever found
brachiopods here. Show me where you found it and I'll record it in the
fossil record, tagged with your name."

In those days, the geologic map of Alaska was incomplete with vast
tracks of land waiting to be charted. With so much of the wealth of
the state tied up in natural resources, it was vital to fill in the gaps. We
knew deposits of oil and natural gas, gold, and other metals awaited
discovery. Finding them would be vital to the struggling economy
of the state. And with the Cold War brewing, we knew that key new
deposits could become crucial to the defense of the entire country—
perhaps the western world at large. To find them, those vast empty
swathes on the geological map had to be filled in. It was a monumental
task.

Yet here I was, before classes even started, already making a
contribution to the world's knowledge of the all-important puzzle that
was Alaska's geological terrain. If I had any lingering doubts about
becoming a geologist, they disappeared right there, like that long-
departed sea.

The first night, we set up our camp next to a dry river bed. After
the nylon tents went up, I took a walk and found remnants of wildlife—
eagle feathers and a perfectly spiraled mountain sheep's horn. I learned
that you could tell the age of the sheep by the degree of curl. This one
had come from an old rutting ram. I felt like the north was opening

up to me, whispering its secrets, allowing me to peer into its soul.

By the time we had a quick meal and cleaned up the campsite, the temperature had plummeted. We crawled into the tents, too cold to change our clothes. I wrapped myself in the blankets, like a mummy, but even so I went to sleep shivering. In the morning I woke up still trembling from the cold. I didn't realize that I could shiver all night and sleep through it. I was learning that to become a geological explorer, I would have to push my body to its limits, and find out where those boundaries were.

By the second night, we'd moved north of the Brooks Range onto the North Slope, the vast plains that flattened down to the Arctic Ocean. We camped on the broad tundra flats near Toolik, where the tundra was made up of springy twigs and reindeer moss that erupted from the ground in vibrant shades of orange and red. Above us, the vast twilight sky turned a luminous pink and seemed to stretch forever, making us feel small. The rising pearlescent moon, fat and full, lit up the tundra like a sea of blood under a salmon-colored sky. Having studied earth science and our planet's place in the solar system, we all were struck by the same thought—that this landscape didn't seem to belong on Earth; it looked like the surface of Mars.

Wordless and humbled, I drank in this sight for a long time, in absolute awe that the real Alaska was bigger than my dream.

5.

✧ Amazing Grace ✧

𝒯HE NEXT DAY WE HEADED BACK DOWN the Haul Road, returning to Fairbanks just in time for registration. Students scrambled to get a place in their preferred classes. At most universities, this chore is as frustrating as a long line for the ladies' room—but not here. The Engineering Department had built a Darth Vader suit, worn by a fellow who walked among us while another took Polaroid snapshots of students posing with Darth. The first photo I sent home to my family was of me shaking hands with the Dark Lord himself. It wasn't what my parents expected, but like me, they would learn that things were different in Fairbanks.

I signed up for calculus, geochemistry, and geomorphology, a subject that was hard for me to even pronounce. For the most part, that first term went by in a migraine blur. But there was one class that I never would forget. It was the field-methods class, designed to prepare us for working in the bush. After two terms of studying field methods, we were to apply our knowledge the following summer in a six-week mapping program. Most conventional field programs send students to areas that already have been mapped. There, the students can check their fledgling mapping skills against what the experts already know. But this was Alaska, and with so much land not yet explored, our summer field camp would map an uncharted region. We wouldn't just be students; we would be active contributors to the map of the region.

First, however, we would spend the fall and spring terms practicing with the tools we would need. We would learn how to use a transit for surveying, stereoscopes for aerial photo interpretation, and the precise compasses that didn't merely measure magnetic north (somewhere in Canada) but could be adjusted, depending on your latitude, for true north.

The first day, Dr. Payne introduced us to the equipment, outlining it all on the blackboard. While we dutifully took notes, I could hear a clomping noise coming from the stairwell at the end of the hall. The commotion, a cross between a thud and a shuffle, got louder as it echoed in the hallway. The noise increased until the professor could no longer ignore it. One student smiled and said, "The Amazing Grace is back."

The amazing who? Back from where? Whoever this Bigfoot was, he sure made a lot of racket.

The footsteps approached the classroom door and then stopped. As all heads turned, in walked a slip of a girl in her late teens with a cascade of chocolate brown hair that was longer than her denim miniskirt. Her legs were bare, emerging from wide heavy boots that looked two sizes too big. The boots were padded with felt liners, and she wore them without socks. Her shoe laces, undone, dragged behind her forcing the boots to flop around on her bare ankles, each step slapping the floor: *ka-clunk, ka-clunk, ka-chunk.*

"I'm late?" she asked, as if she didn't know. "Oh, I'm sorry. I'm sorry, I'm so sorry. I'm really, really so sorry."

Dr. Payne waited for her to take a seat. She took his silence as an opportunity to issue another burst of apologies. But the more she apologized, the more flustered she became until she had worked herself into such a frenzy of embarrassment that she knocked a glass beaker onto the floor. As the shards scattered, she was spurred to yet a new wave of apologies.

"I'm really awfully sorry. Oh, this is terrible and I'm so sorry. I really am. Oh, what a bad Yvonne I am—bad, bad."

Then she sat down. But what about the glass? She seemed torn, as if she should do something about it.

She jumped up and spun around, her arms flailing. But the teacher needed to resume. So she sat down again. Then up again, then down. I couldn't believe my eyes. I was riveted as she bounced up and down with no end in sight.

The whole room watched, transfixed, except for a guy with curly hair who found a paper towel and calmly scooped up the glass.

"Oh, thank you," she said, sitting down for the last time. "Thank you, thank you, thank you. I really am sorry about all of this."

Bemused, Dr. Payne resumed his lecture.

By then I was unable to concentrate. I had attended hundreds, possibly thousands of classes, but I never had seen an entrance like that. My thoughts were stuck on the outlandish girl who had turned a mundane Monday morning class introduction into an event.

I could guess the "amazing" part of her name, but it wasn't until later that I found out she was Yvonne Grace. I wondered how our paths would cross, what part in my new life she might play.

I didn't yet know that she would become a life-long friend, or that the no-nonsense guy who picked up the glass would become even more.

～～

After the first week of the term, a big party was held for faculty and students at Dr. Stone's house. The Stone family lived in a cedar A-frame with a sweeping view of the Tanana Valley at the end of a long, twisting road. I looked forward to getting off campus and seeing how Alaskans lived. But I was excited for another reason. As I got ready for the party, my roommate, who was preparing for a dinner date, asked me where I was going.

"I'm going to a party," I said, "where I'll meet my life-long partner."

She thought I was joking. I wasn't. Something inside me told me it was true. I couldn't explain it, but it was a feeling as strong as the one that brought me north.

In the kitchen of Dr. Stone's home, by the bowl of potato chips, I saw the curly-haired guy I'd noticed during Dr. Payne's lecture. He noticed me too and, within ten minutes of walking in the door, I was in a deep conversation with Tom Albanese that didn't want to end.

And it didn't. The more I found out about him, the more I was drawn in. We were similar in a lot of ways, both raised on the East Coast. We were close with our families even though our lives brought us here. As kids, we both had read every scrap of science we could find, devouring the family encyclopedia and then reading our way through the school library, until our hometown didn't fit anymore. Neither of us could explain to our families why we had gone to Alaska and we couldn't explain it to anyone else either. People often asked me why I had gone north, but I never had a short answer that made sense. With

Tom I didn't have to explain. We just *knew*. How good it was to find someone who doesn't have to ask who you are because they already get it.

I had taken on an advanced geology degree, despite the requisite coursework I still needed. Tom had done something even more ambitious. Torn between studying mining engineering and economics, he had combined the two to form his own program, a degree in mineral economics. Then he got the degree approved by the board of regents. It was a bold move. He was perhaps the only student in the university history to devise and get approval for a new program that he tailor-made to suit his own goals.

As I had seen that first day, Tom was a person who got things done. He wasn't afraid of hard work and could assess a situation with a cool eye. Once he knew what was needed, it would happen. Defeat wasn't an option; the job would get done.

Like me, he had an artistic side, too. On his wall was a series of his pen and ink sketches of his climbing adventures, with tiny mountaineers making their way up vast snowy vistas, evoking a mood of respect for the world of ice and snow.

As an undergraduate, Tom was a few years younger than I but had already worked two summers in the field. With sparkling eyes that flashed with a hint of mischief, his cup wasn't half full; it was almost always spilling over with a joy for life that was positively infectious. There was something serious between us right from the start, and as the fall nights grew longer, you would be hard-pressed to find anything more romantic than long walks under a cobalt black sky, electrified by the dancing green flames of the northern lights.

One of my courses was a one-week rock-climbing class. It made sense to learn the basics of ropes and carabiners if I was going to work in the mountains. Tom was already a serious climber. So, on one of our early dates, we decided to go on a climb together. It seemed like a good idea at the time.

It was late September and the cold weather had started to settle in, turning the higher elevations into snow and ice. We planned to climb up a frozen waterfall. It sounded enchanting.

A few hours south on the Parks Highway, we arrived at the cliff where a wall of frozen water gleamed in the sun. We strapped on the crampons, the metal teeth you clamp onto your boots, and started up the wall of ice with an ice ax in each hand.

In ice climbing, your entire weight is supported by your toe-holds, balanced by the grips with your ice axes. We worked our way up, clinging to the most tenuous surfaces with toe spikes and ice axes, no part of our bodies actually touching the ice wall. The effort was grueling; in ice climbing, gravity is not your friend. When we got one-third of the way up, the trickle of ice began to crumble.

We scaled back down safely, but my legs were burning. I thought I must have been doing something wrong.

"No," said Tom. "That's exactly how it's supposed to feel, with your calves screaming in pain."

"It's supposed to hurt?" I asked. "Where's the fun part?"

Tom thought about it and agreed that ice-climbing was a sport that gave you a remarkable sense of achievement—but only *after* the climb. It was hideously painful when you were climbing. He suggested we try a snow climb instead.

A week later, we joined a group of his climber friends on a trip south to a mountain called Panorama Peak. Nestled in a pristine wilderness, the snow-capped mountain towered over everything around it. We strapped on our gear and hiked up the base.

The snow made the rocks slippery. I asked Tom what to do if I slipped.

"That's easy," he said. "You dig in with your ice ax and stop yourself." To demonstrate, he plopped down and began sliding down the slope, then dug in using his ax like a brake.

I tried it; it was great fun sliding down the white slope like a seal, slip-sliding in the sea of snow.

As the terrain became steeper, we were forced to use our hands to pull ourselves up. The hand-holds became wetter as the sun gently melted the snow. We continued on, each bit of progress hard won as we negotiated the snow-covered face. I found I could climb it, but not very fast. This was no surprise since my natural pace, whether walking or hiking, has never been fast. The rest of the group went up above us while Tom stayed with me.

As we worked our way up, I lost all sense of time. All I could think about was the next hold, and then the next, as the pointed peak of the summit loomed closer and closer.

Then, just when it looked as if we'd make it to the top, Tom said we should start back down.

"Why?" I asked. "We'll be at the top soon."

"We don't have time," he said. "To catch our ride back home, we'll have to start back down now because climbing down is just as hard as climbing up, and takes just as much time."

"What do you mean?" I said. "Don't we just slide down and dig in with our ice ax when we want to stop?"

"Don't do that!" he said.

"Why? Didn't you say we could just…?"

"That was at the bottom," he said, "where the slope wasn't so steep. We've gone past that point hours ago. If you slip here, you'll be going too fast."

"My ice ax won't stop me?"

"No," he said. "Slip here and you'll die."

Did he really say that? Yes, and he meant it. Somehow my recreational outing had turned into a life-or-death situation. We started down, and it soon became obvious that Tom was wrong about one thing. Climbing down was not as hard as climbing up; it was much harder. On the way down, the added weight of your downward momentum works against you. A toe-hold strong enough to anchor your weight heading up might give way when your foot's moving down. Your leading holds are not at eye-level but are down by your feet. Toe-holds are harder to see, but what you can't miss are the rocks far below you. Forced to look down, you can't help but see how far you will fall if you slip.

By now, I was not enjoying any part of this. We had been climbing for hours and my legs started to cramp. Then they started shaking and refused to go any farther. And I refused, too.

"I'm done," I said to Tom. "I'm staying right here."

"You can't do that," said Tom. "We have to get down and catch our ride."

"You go catch it," I said. "I'm not going anywhere. I'm fine right here."

Of course I wasn't fine. There was nothing fine about any of this.

Tom wasn't about to leave me up there, and persisted with reason. Eventually I had to agree; I had to climb down.

With my legs still shaking, I reached down to find one more foothold, then another. The sun was low when we finally reached the base and joined the rest of the guys who had made it to the top *and* beat us down.

As we drove back to town, the climbers erupted with stories of the day's exploits, their eyes shining and red, drunk on adrenaline as they recounted every detail. They had seen the world from the top and having cheated death once again, they laughed in its face. It seemed to me that as with ice-climbing, the best part of snow-climbing was the part that came after, not the sport itself.

I couldn't share their joy. I didn't feel triumphant to have survived all that danger—I felt stupid to have put myself in it. As a geologist, I knew I would have to go up hills and mountains, some of them steep. But I decided then and there that this would be my last recreational climb. I thought Tom would be disappointed when I told him, but he wasn't. Instead, he agreed that climbing was dangerous, and frankly, he wasn't enjoying it much anymore, either. He had lost good friends in climbing accidents, young men who didn't need to die. Now that Tom had a girlfriend, he realized there were plenty of other ways to enjoy his life without risking it, so he quit climbing, too.

I appreciated his attitude, that he had the confidence and maturity to walk away from it without regrets. He didn't have to prove himself.

Tom's climbing buddies, however, weren't happy with his decision. Two days after we returned from Panorama Peak, I was walking across the campus when Yvonne Grace came running up, her boots flapping, breathless with news.

"You'll never guess what I heard," she gasped. "There's a rumor that Tom Albanese is dating an older woman! Can you believe it? All the guys are talking about it. What do you think? Could it be true?"

"I'm sure of it," I said. "He's dating me, and I'm three years older."

Then something rare happened. The Amazing Grace went silent. With her foot so firmly jammed down her mouth, she had no idea how to get it out.

As her face turned red, I had to laugh. Of course Tom's friends were annoyed. He was outgrowing their boyish stunts.

At the same time, I was pleased. I was afraid Tom's friends thought of me as that ridiculously slow climber. But now I knew the truth. To them, I was something else entirely—the wicked older woman. It was a much better title, and I couldn't help but laugh.

Yvonne was stunned, then confused that I wasn't upset. This was a new experience for her. She had displayed her amazing talent to say the wrong thing to the wrong person. But it hadn't gotten her into trouble this time.

Her face wrinkled as she pondered this, and I laughed even more. I liked the uncensored Yvonne, despite her blunders, or maybe because of them. For me, given the choice between blunt truth or flattery, I'll take truth any day.

6.

⤚ McKinley Retreat ⤚

ONE OF TOM'S CLIMBER FRIENDS didn't mind Tom's new social life. In the same month Tom and I started dating, Vaughn Hoeffler, a chemistry student with shiny dark hair, a gift from his mother's Alaska native heritage, also met someone special. She was Carol Fuiten, a chemistry freshman who was in one of my labs. With swinging blonde hair and a dazzling smile, she reminded me of Joni Mitchell. Although Carol looked like a California blonde, she grew up in Alaska and told amazing stories of living by herself as a teenager in a log cabin near Denali. When a bear ripped off the cabin's door, all she had to defend herself with was a cast-iron frying pan. To look at this care-free girl, you would never believe she possessed such inner steel.

That fall, the four of us went double-dating, enjoying whatever entertainment the campus could offer. We went on movie nights or caught shows on one of the few campus TVs in a dorm lounge with a dozen students all sitting around watching the same little screen. Sometimes we listened to guest speakers including Gene Roddenberry, executive producer of the television series *Star Trek*. He swaggered onto the stage and told brilliant stories about creating his "Wagon Train to the Stars" and making it come to life on the screen. I understood what he was trying to achieve. As a fledgling explorer myself, I was seeking a bold future, too.

For Thanksgiving that year, the four of us decided to spend the holiday break at the cabin Carol's family still owned in the wilderness near Mount McKinley National Park (renamed Denali National Park in 1980). The cabin had no electricity, phone, or plumbing. It had a woodstove for cooking and heating and an outhouse out back. From the Parks Highway, we would have to ski in with supplies for five days strapped to our backs.

Carol and Vaughn had grown up in Alaska and were cross-country skiers. Tom was as well, but I had never been on skis before. Tom said not to worry, you just strap them on and shuffle your feet as if you were ice-skating. That was the only lesson I would get. It seemed good enough. In those heady days, everything seemed possible. Nothing could stop us; nothing felt beyond my grasp.

The four of us scrounged up the gear, borrowed a car, and headed south. Four hours later we came to a mountain pass. We shoveled into a snowbank on the side of the road to make space for the car. It was barely three o'clock but already twilight. The midnight sun of the summer was long gone, and every day we were losing six minutes of daylight. By Thanksgiving, the darkness lingered for nineteen hours a day. In the short time it took us to park the car and strap on our gear, we were swallowed in night.

I knew that cross-country skiing with packs would be hard on my legs, but I hadn't realized how much-upper body effort was required to push and pull with the ski poles. Despite the cold, it wasn't long before we were steaming with sweat as we slid away into the shadowed blankets of snow.

Tom was right; the motion was like ice-skating on planks and I found myself skiing along. As usual, I was the slowest and the last in the line.

We skied through a small gully with hills of dark forests on both sides, dwarfed by the surroundings, like four little ants with big humps on our backs. The snow all around us muffled the sounds. All I could hear was my own breathing, hard and deep, and the long swish of the ski blades against the icy ground.

Up ahead, one after another, the others cut to the left and disappeared from view. When I got there myself, I saw a vista that stopped me cold. By this time I had seen magnificent sights in Alaska and had come to take the scenery for granted. But I couldn't ignore this as I found myself standing on the edge of a cliff high above the Nenana River, a wide ribbon of ice that stretched for miles below. Beyond the river, the peaks of the Alaska Range gleamed like polished silver in the moonlight, so jagged and sharp they looked as if they had been cut in place by God's scissors.

Sitting proud on the bluff was a perfect log cabin that looked over the river with a stained-glass window that sparkled like a jeweled kaleidoscope.

I stood there drinking in the sight, riveted in place until the sweat on my cheeks felt like ice needles were forming, a reminder that I had things to do.

Inside, we started a fire and unloaded our gear. For the next few days, everything required effort. Snow had to be melted for our water, and cooking on top of the woodstove demanded patience and skill. Even a trip to the outhouse was a chore requiring layers of protection before stomping outside to expose tender skin to the searing cold.

Still, those five days at the cabin were unforgettably delicious. When the sun finally came up on the second day, we made our way down the cliff to the frozen river, skiing every minute of those precious four or five hours of daylight. When night fell, we returned to the cabin, ravenously hungry, and ate mountains of pancakes and eggs, washed down with kettles of hot chocolate. With our stomachs stretched tight, we would climb the ladder to the rafters where our beds awaited, cotton quilts layered thick on the plank floor, and sleep the long night away.

When morning arrived, nineteen hours later, we would come down from the loft and start the pattern all over again.

Away from clocks and artificial light, I was surprised to see how quickly our bodies adapted to the rhythms of nature, with the short days filled with robust activity, followed by the long nights spent hibernating like bears. It was such a raw, primal feeling to toss away accepted human patterns and embrace the sun cycle, however skewed it was. I thought it would feel strange, but it seemed like the most natural thing in the world—not the world of man, but the real world of snow and shadows and ice.

At the end of the week, when the hot chocolate ran out, it was time to go back to the world of classes and teachers and school.

⌒

After Tom gave up climbing, he started an exploration company with four friends who were all working on mining-related degrees. They called their company the Cosmic Oyster Mining Company, or Comco for short. The brain of the operation was Karl Hanneman, a tall Nordic skier who wore shattered black glasses stuck together with medical tape. The first time I saw him with his busted geek glasses, he was hobbling on crutches thanks to a ski injury. Not that breaking his leg slowed him down, or kept him from joining this ambitious group. Next was big Ron Brooks, a long-time Alaskan, full of energy with shoulders like a Mack truck; he was the brawn. The wit of the team was Joe Head, a wiry redneck cowboy whose clever words came out slow and twangy in his country drawl. He was the one who had come up with the company name. And rounding it out was Tom, who supplied the drive with his seemingly effortless way of getting things done. These guys pooled their talents to find areas ripe for mining deposits. Then they went out and secured the mineral rights by staking their claims.

Staking a claim is just as it sounds: You go to the site and pound stakes into the corners of every acre. Registering the claim back in town grants you the mineral rights to that land for one year.

At that time, several mining companies were combing the state, eager to find the next big deposit. And for every sniff of a discovery, the Comco boys were on it. They didn't have the resources that the big companies did—no helicopters, no big budget, and no crew. They were just this handful of college boys who rented a truck, drove as far as they could, and hiked the rest of the way in. Still, sometimes they beat the big companies to a find.

One day the Comco partners got a hot tip and shot out of campus to stake new claims. That evening, I waited in the cafeteria, wondering if the guys would make it back before the dining hall closed at 8 p.m. There was no other place to eat on campus, and I knew they wouldn't be happy if they missed their dinner.

Minutes before closing, as the staff began taking away the food trays, a distant rumbling noise outside grew louder and louder until a helicopter landed on the cafeteria roof.

It was Tom and his Comco friends, who burst in from the upstairs terrace and raced to the food counter, loading their plates seconds before the big double doors were locked for the night. As they consumed huge helpings of food, Tom explained how they had staked a claim right under the nose of a major company that wanted those rights. When the company's manager found that these enterprising young men had beat him to it, he was so impressed that he offered them jobs.

"Only if you get us back to campus before the cafeteria closes" was Joe's cheeky reply. "We are not missing our dinner."

Charmed by their good-natured bravado, the company official flew them back. This was probably the only time on campus that students literally dropped in for dinner.

This was one of the many reasons that we felt we were on top of the world. We were! One time, I heard Joe's novel explanation of a map of the United States to a child.

"Up here is Alaska where all the cool people live," he said. "Down here is Hawaii, where all the cool people go on vacation. In between is everything else, where all the boring people live."

I laughed as he said it, but the truth is, we all felt that way. We lived where anything was possible, where the unimaginable could happen, and quite often did.

As I would discover, not all of those things were good.

7.

ᔈ Dead of Winter ᔈ

AFTER THANKSGIVING, IT WAS HARD TO BELIEVE that the nights would get even longer. But they did. In the days before Christmas, the sun didn't show itself until shortly before noon. Even then it would only limp across the horizon for a couple of hours before slipping away.

That December the weather dropped to 20 F (-7 C) and then down to a frigid -10 F (-23 C). Having grown up in the snow belt of the Great Lakes, I had experienced these temperatures. I thought I knew all about cold weather and didn't believe it could *feel* any colder than this.

I was wrong. As the temperature continued to drop, I was in for a whole new level of sub-zero, hyper-cold experience.

Most people consider freezing temperature to be cold. Water freezes at 32 Fahrenheit (0 Centigrade), which in Alaska, is just the threshold of cold weather. This is what I learned:

At 0 F (-18 C), the cold feels bitter. You can get frostbite and damage your skin without a thick layer of winter gear.

At -20 F (-29 C), the air is so cold that it hurts to breathe in. If you breathe too fast, your lungs are at risk from freezer burn. At these temperatures, you need double layers of everything. Without insulated boots, you could lose your toes. Without two pairs of mittens, your fingers will turn numb. If you ignore that warning sign, you could lose them.

It gets worse. At around -30 F (-34 C), the thin mucus lining of your nose freezes solid. One friend could actually hear a "click" when his nose froze solid. At this point, you are forced to breathe through your mouth. This injects cold air into the lungs faster. To protect my lungs at these temperatures, I breathed through a thick wool scarf.

At -40 F (-40 C), the cold is as far from body temperature as the boiling point, and the effect on the body is much the same. Skin exposed to air at this temperature feels as if it's been splashed with scalding water. The effect is just as painful and potentially damaging. There are few second chances. If you get it wrong, if you try to beat the cold without proper winter dress, expect to pay the price.

All this makes life complicated. Not just managing your body, but also getting around in sub-zero conditions. Vehicles behave differently at these temperatures, too.

First, the rubber in the tires freezes solid. The slightly flattened part, where the tire rests on the ground, freezes into this shape so the tire is no longer entirely round. With every revolution, the tire clunks and shakes, threatening to split apart. This is known as the square-tire effect.

At extreme cold, metal becomes brittle. I have been in more than one car when a door was slammed shut by a novice Alaskan. In normal temperatures, this is standard procedure. In sub-below conditions, you risk shattering the lock or breaking the door.

Ron Brooks from Tom's Comco group had a pickup truck with a tricky door that refused to stay closed past a certain temperature. The metal catch simply refused to grip and the door would swing open at exactly -35 F (-37 C). One winter day, Tom was riding in Ron's truck when the door sprang wide open, nearly ejecting Tom from the passenger seat.

"Sorry about that," said Ron. "That door always pops open at thirty-five below."

When they drove past a bank with an outdoor temperature display, sure enough, the temperature read exactly -35 F.

Our cars were fitted with electric battery blankets and oil-pan heaters, and we drove around with an electrical plug sticking out of the hood. Parking lots had electric outlets. When the weather dropped, if you forgot to plug in, you could forget about starting the car.

In most places, a power outage is a nuisance. In extreme cold, it's a nightmare. One cold night a friend's power went out. By morning, it still hadn't been restored. With no heat his water pipes froze and ruptured. He was desperate to get out for supplies but of course, his car wouldn't start. He tried to warm his car with the only source of heat he could find, a gasoline-powered weed burner. Long story short: his car went up in a ball of flames.

A lot of folks kept a spare bag of winter clothes in their garage or storage shed. If a fire or some other emergency flushed you out of the house, you could make it to a neighbor's house for help without losing your toes.

In those dead winter months, it might stay under -30 F (-34 C) for weeks at a time. As we went about our business, every trip outside was an effort. If you forgot one piece of your protective gear, or didn't realize the weather had dropped, you could be in trouble.

It was unalaskan to pass by without offering to help when someone was stranded in cold weather. If my car broke down alongside the road, the next motorist invariably stopped. Fairbanks prided itself on being called the "Golden Heart City" and not just because of the gold.

The cold bonded us. We were all in this together. With a spirit like that, it was a little easier to make it through to the spring.

8.

≈ Thesis Blues ≈

$\mathcal{S}$OMEONE TOLD ME THAT WHEN THE WORST of winter receded, and temperatures rose to 20 degrees (-7 C), people in Fairbanks would venture outside in tee-shirts and sneakers. I didn't believe it at first but it was true. Although it was still colder than the freezing point, I shed my winter coat and found myself out dancing in the bright spring sun like everyone else. It felt so liberating to be able to walk unencumbered by all those layers.

I had survived my first winter. By pushing my brain as far as it would go, I had survived my first semester, too, and passed the first round of classes I had worried about.

However, I was starting to realize that the classes, no matter how difficult, were baby steps compared to what lay ahead—the thesis. I learned why so many students feared it. A thesis was not just a long essay; it was where you proved your expertise in your topic. Because so much of Alaska's geology was unmapped, you wouldn't become a mere expert, you were expected to become *the world's leading authority* on that particular niche.

There were the practical matters to consider, too. Just getting to your study site was an ordeal in Alaska, with the few roads and even fewer airstrips. Then there was the matter of paying for your expedition. At the time, I couldn't even afford a used car.

It was an endurance test with so many tasks, every one of them daunting, every one able to defeat you. More than half of the graduate students dropped out of the program before ever laying eyes on their rocks. Even completing the field work was no guarantee. I watched second- and third-year students who had finished their field work but were stumped by their data and dropped out in defeat.

Due to the physical rigors of field work, the attrition rate was even higher among the women. In a school with a few thousand students, I watched one woman after another bail out of the program (including Rita from my Brooks Range trip) until I could count the number of female graduate students on one hand.

As I took all this in, I tried not to think of the ones who just turned up missing, too embarrassed to say goodbye when they left for the Lower 48. I couldn't afford to dwell on that. I needed to focus on what I had to do.

The first step was to conceive of a project that would define my specialty field and area of expertise. As a failed teacher-trainee with a watered-down geology background, I wondered how I was supposed to do that.

Had I bitten off more than I could chew? I wanted this new life, but it was hard keeping my doubts at bay.

One day after a lecture in March, Dr. "Tripp" Triplehorn, the sedimentology professor who had saved my Brooks Range trip the first week of school, posted some questions on the blackboards that were not part of his lecture. One question caught my attention. In the Alaska Range, Tripp said, there were three formations of igneous rocks (cooled from a molten phase) about twenty miles (32 km) apart. If they were related, what could that tell us about what was going on beneath the surface?

Unable to find any information about those rocks, I flagged down Dr. Tripp in the hall a few days later.

"About those three igneous formations in the Alaska Range," I said. "I can't tell if they're related. There's nothing written on them. No samples, no dates. So what's the story? Are they part of the same magma event or not?"

"How would I know?" he said. "I work with sediments. You're the one interested in these igneous rocks. You go figure it out."

I was intrigued. There was something primal about rocks born of fire and heat that made me want to know more. Unlike sedimentary rocks that were reformed from dirt, or metamorphic rocks that have been squeezed into shape, igneous rocks have been cooled from a melt, leaving clues of their fiery birth frozen in place in their crystalline structure. If you understood how to read these clues, they would give you their secrets—the depth of the melt, direction of flow, and the type of gases trapped inside. Measuring the tiny traces of radioactive decay, they might even whisper their age. I didn't yet know how to read these clues, but I wanted to find out.

I wanted to see those rocks Dr. Tripp had asked about, and discover their history. This became my thesis topic. From then on, these were *my* rocks. Once again, Dr. Tripp had come to my rescue. Now I had a specialty to pursue and a target area to explore. I would become an igneous geologist.

There was a small problem. The Geology Department didn't have an igneous geologist on the staff but planned to hire someone the following year.

In the meantime, I could spend the summer learning about field work. For the first half of the summer, I would be doing my field camp course. Our class would map a spot in the Brooks Range. I looked forward to going back into those mountains that had lured me into geology, this time not as a visitor but as a resident, at least for six weeks.

For the second half of the summer, I hoped to get a field job with an exploration company. I needed all the field experience I could get. In those days, summer field jobs were easy to find. Exploration companies came to our campus eager to fill their seasonal crews with cheap student labor. We got training and the companies got employees who understood the rigors of working in the wilderness.

That spring when the companies came to campus, every geology student I knew was offered a summer job—everyone but me. This was maddening. Once again, in a field desperate for employees, I was left out.

Looking into it, I found that one of the professors had mistakenly told the recruiters I wasn't available. He thought I would be tied up doing field research for my thesis. But that wasn't my plan. I wasn't ready to start that work. How could I begin my own research as an igneous geologist without expert guidance? But by the time I discovered the mix-up, all the jobs were taken. This meant that after field camp, I would have six weeks of summer with nothing to do—unless I revised my plan.

For a geologist in Alaska, where snow covers the ground nine months a year, the three months of summer are too precious to waste. I wondered if I could start my thesis field work that year after all. If so, I would have to step up the pace. Everything I had expected to learn over the next fifteen months would have to be crammed into a few weeks, and without benefit of a mentor.

This seemed impossible. But once the idea took hold, I knew I had to try. In the rashness of youth, I was guided by an ethic that didn't seem to make sense but somehow felt right for me—*if at first you don't succeed, try something that's harder.*

9.

⁖ Deals within Deals ⁖

_I_ NEEDED TO LEARN HOW TO READ MY ROCKS—what to look for, what to collect, and how to collect it. I would only be there once. There was no room for finding out later there was something else I should have done.

The subject of igneous rocks was broad, including volcanoes that spewed onto the surface and intrusive rocks that had cooled underground. Locating the magma pipes and sub-surface features required geophysical modeling. One professor helpfully told me I must also become an "instant expert" on geochronology, the study of rock-dating techniques. The list of my expertise requirements grew with mind-boggling speed.

I went around campus seeking out every geologist I could find with knowledge of these subjects, relentlessly asking questions, soaking up information.

On the main campus, Dr. Stone loaned me a magnetometer and showed me how to conduct a magnetic survey for mapping the shape of the magma pipe below ground.

Up on the West Ridge I found Dr. Juergen Kienle, a volcanologist so passionate about his work that he once lowered himself down into the caldera of an active volcano to collect super-fresh samples. Dr. Kienle was enthusiastic about my project and directed me to the latest research on eruptive events. He even agreed to become one of my thesis advisers.

Tapping the university's pool of knowledge was a good start but it wasn't enough. I spoke to government geologists at branches of the U.S. Bureau of Mines, the U.S. Geological Survey, and most important of all, the Alaska State Survey, officially known as the Division of Geological and Geophysical Surveys. If anyone knew about mapping Alaska, these guys did. It was their mission to map the geology of the state.

Most of them generously shared what they knew. One state geologist in particular, Tom Bundtzen, was a virtual encyclopedia of knowledge. With his Sherlock Holmes hat and a field lens always at hand, he looked like a detective in search of clues. From Bundtzen I learned that a geologist really is a detective. The trick to solving the mystery is often in asking the right questions.

Slowly, I pieced together a master plan listing each phase of the field work and how much time the various aspects should take. I trimmed my budget as tight as I could, but with lab costs the expenses would total a whopping twenty-three-hundred dollars. Some mining companies funded student research but only if the rocks were likely to host economic minerals. My rocks were not good candidates for mineral deposits.

Someone suggested I speak to Dr. Don Turner, a research scientist who had a grant from the U.S. Department of Energy to investigate sources of geothermal energy. Dr. Turner was a towering presence, well over six feet tall, with intense eyes and a Rasputin stare. As far as I knew, he had never sponsored a graduate student. It was a daunting prospect to enter the labyrinth of research high up in Geophysical Institute and knock on his door.

To my surprise, he was intrigued by the fiery birth of my rocks and the possibility that they might point to a source of geothermal heat. He even agreed to become my main thesis advisor.

We made a deal. Dr. Turner would fund my project with a fraction of his Department of Energy grant. In exchange, after my field work was done, I would work for him, compiling and drafting a massive, comprehensive map of Alaska's geothermal resources, the first of its kind. Suddenly, not only did I have funding, but I would also get hands-on experience making maps. In those days before computers, all the maps were drafted by hand. Drafting was a precise and delicate skill that frustrated and eluded a lot of my male counterparts. But I liked to draw. Maybe all those art classes were going to pay off after all.

Up at the Alaska survey, Tom Bundtzen steered me to a well-known state geologist, Holister Grant, who had published a geology book and was planning to work near my area that summer with a helicopter crew. I was apprehensive about meeting him. After all, he was an author and I was a first-year grad student without a day of real field experience.

I found Holister in his office leaning over a light table, staring bleary-eyed at a tattered field map. He seemed to welcome a break from it and was intrigued that I would be working near his camp. Then he came up with an idea. If I agreed to publish my findings in one of the Alaska survey's scientific journals, I could use his helicopter to get around when his ground crew didn't need it.

I could hardly believe my luck. But when we compared our field schedules, they didn't overlap. My spirits sank. He planned to work in the Alaska Range the first half of the summer when I would be up north in my field camp in the Brooks Range. By the time I was finished there, Holister's camp and helicopter crew would have left the Alaska Range.

Then Holister came up with another idea. Before I went off to field camp, he would fly me around for a day. I could visit each of my three rock formations for a preliminary look around and drop off equipment and caches of food. Then, when I hiked back in for my exploration later in the summer, I would have much less weight to carry.

This would help, but I had no idea how to store and protect food against wild animals. For that, Holister sent me to see Dr. John Dillon, the Brooks Range expert with the firecrackers. Dillon was investigating food containers for his own upcoming expedition and had found a company that made heavy plastic thirty-gallon barrels with strong screw-top lids. They were waterproof and, he hoped, air-tight enough to keep the bears from smelling the food. But they were expensive, and I needed three. We came up with a plan. If I bought him one barrel, Dillon would lend me three. I was learning that one of the most important skills for exploration work was the art of making deals.

As summer approached, I stuffed the three barrels with dry food, carefully portioned in zip-lock bags. Dry food was cheaper than canned food and easier to pack. My menu was boringly bland—oatmeal, dried beans, and noodles. For the protein that we would need to keep our strength up, I added a few sacks of freeze-dried protein nuggets. The climbers swore by this stuff, although it smelled like dog food and tasted like cardboard. No matter. It didn't cost much and I wasn't expecting gourmet dining.

The spring semester drew to a close. Tom went off to Southeast Alaska to work for Anaconda, a mining company exploring for mineral deposits. It was the first of many summers we spent apart working in different parts of the state. Tom had worked for this company before and knew what to expect. But this would be my first summer working in the field. If I messed it up, my geology career would be over.

When the dorms closed for the summer, I had to find a place to stay between trips. Of course it had to be cheap. It was time to make another deal.

A short walk from campus was a place called the Sandvik House, where the head of the Alpine Club lived. Doug Buchanan was a gregarious man with a big bushy beard and a head of mad curls. Because of his high-octane enthusiasm for the outdoors, the Sandvik House became the nucleus of the climbing world and was usually stuffed with people. The hard-core adventurers came here for camaraderie and to show off their latest mountaineering, kayaking, or parachuting adventures with stunning slide-shows held twice a week. The front hall was lined with stretchers and body bags from the various rescue missions, not always successful. On any given day, you could wander through the living room and find three or four people napping on giant bean-bag chairs or someone sleeping in the pull-down shelf over the toilet.

Our double-dating friends Carol and Vaughn had moved off-campus and rented a room in the Sandvik House. They would be away for a while so I sub-let their room for the two weeks before field camp started. It was here among the intense life-or-death world of climbers that I planned for my first summer in the Alaskan wilderness.

Of all the adrenalin junkies I met there who offered tips on surviving in the wild, one who seemed marked for a special destiny was Johnny Waterman, a sturdy, compact climber who did something no one else did. He made the big ascents that required ropes and oxygen tanks but he climbed solo. Despite climbing alone, he managed to return with outrageous photographs of himself swinging from a rope over some murderous precipice, his feet dangling in the air over thousand-foot drops.

To get these photos, he had to climb up onto a ledge, anchor his camera into the snow with the timer set, and then climb up onto an opposite ledge and swing back and forth, taking multiple shots in hopes that some would catch him in the frame. This required prodigious amounts of gear and film. On one climb, he carried seven backpacks of equipment, which meant he had to go up and down each treacherous pitch seven times.

I worried about Johnny, especially when he began talking about his invisible climbing companion, Pierre. During one slide show, he told us Pierre had led the ascent and "taught me zee French, oui oui?" After that, I no longer could enjoy his photos, as astonishing as they were, or encourage his climbing compulsion. The climbers lived precariously close to the edge but Johnny was dancing on it. Whenever he dropped by I would say, "It's good to see you," but what I felt was, *it's good to see you alive.*

Then he attempted a solo winter climb to the summit of Denali. Johnny Waterman (not Jonathan Waterman, the author) went up the mountain and never returned. The rescue teams combed Denali but found no trace of the eccentric climber—not a track, not a hint, not a scrap of gear.

We hoped he would show up somewhere, in a café, in a cabin someplace, as he'd done before. *Surprise! I'm alive!* But he never did. I think of him up there in the snow and the ice, with his camera full of film that no one will see.

Not even Pierre.

10.

A Shotgun Named Sally

AMONG ALL MY LISTS, ONE HAD PRIORITY—my checklist of field dangers. These were the things that could get me injured or killed. Air crashes topped the list. I couldn't prevent those, but there were other hazards I could help to control.

I would need to be vigilant about wild animals. One geologist I knew had been attacked by a rabid fox. It got him one night while he was asleep, biting him through the thin fabric wall of his tent. Another colleague was trampled by a frightened moose. Yet another found himself caught in a musk ox stampede.

The animals that scared me the most were the bears. Nearly everyone I came across had a bear story, told in lurid detail when they learned I was heading into the bush. It was especially hard meeting the geologist who had gone into the same mountain range less than a year before, who now operated her microscope with mechanical hooks. The doctors had tried to save her arms after the bear ripped them off, but it was too late.

I wasn't going to head out into bear country without protection. I wanted something that could stop a full-grown bear. The problem was that with a bear's huge body and massive skull bone, most bullets would only make it angry. I needed a very big gun.

Saving a week's grocery money, I went downtown to a pawn shop and bought an old shotgun that fired slugs as fat as cigars. To prevent it from snagging on the brush (and shooting myself in the leg), I sawed the barrel down to the pump-action stock. This made the shotgun less accurate. If I needed to shoot a bear to save my life, the bear would have to be close; I wouldn't have time to reload.

One of the climbers gave me shooting lessons at a gravel pit. There I learned all about my shotgun—how to take it apart, how to sight in a target, and how to ignore the recoil that slammed into my shoulder. If you flinched at the recoil, it messed up your aim. Old Sally—the name that stuck—kicked like a rocket on steroids.

Once I could hit the target, I felt as prepared as I could be. But was it enough? Bears can run on all fours as fast as a deer. Stopping a charging bear would be very different than hitting tin cans. With my shotgun able to fire one slug at a time, would I be able to squeeze off one perfect, well-timed shot before I was mauled? This was the question that hounded my dreams.

The day finally came to meet my rocks. With Sally slung over my shoulder, I met Holister Grant at the helipad behind the airport. Dr. Kienle was coming, too. I was glad to have his expertise. Our chopper, a Hughes 500-D, looked like a giant mosquito with its bubble head and thin tail. I loaded my three food barrels into the back and strapped myself in for my first helicopter flight.

We wore headphones keyed into microphones, but even with the best sound-proofing technology, I could feel the insistent roar of the rotor blades in every part of my body as the engine powered up.

We lifted straight up off the tarmac, hovering for a moment before the chopper dipped its nose and headed south. For a hundred miles (160 km), we sliced through the air over the mud flats and wide swirls of the Tanana River. When the flats rose into hills, the pilot pulled on the throttle and we skirted up the north flanks of the Alaska Range.

As we flew over the rising ground, I ran my finger along the map, tracing our exact path. It was my first time navigating from the air with a topographic map, one of the many skills required for a field-mapper. The mountains below looked small. From the curved glass of the chopper, the trees and canyons looked like toys. We flew over a spot where a river cut between two cliff banks, and Holister shouted to me over the noise. "That's where Jeff Kline broke his back."

I didn't know who Jeff Kline was, but I made a mental note to add to my checklist of dangers. *Don't fall into a ravine.*

We followed the Totatlanika River to a small tributary called Buzzard Creek. From above, we could see the first of my rock targets, a pair of ponds cut into the side of a mountain, each flanked by a black rubble rim. I suspected these features were a type of volcanic explosion pit known as a maar, formed when rising magma hits the water table and explodes, leaving a lake in the center of a crater pit. Dr. Kienle confirmed this. The mountain that cradled them didn't have a name, so I called these volcanics the Buzzard Creek Maars. To hear Holister and Dr. Kienle use the same term, I realized I had just named these rocks. The magnitude of this gave me chills.

Along the volcanic rim, I collected a few samples, dropped off the surveying gear, and left the first food barrel behind a bush. I would return six weeks later and map the extent and depth of the black cinders that had spewed from the eruption. I would dig below for charred remains, scouring for charcoal and carbon samples to date the age of the blast. Then I would peer even farther below the ground with the geophysical tools.

Then it was time to move on. Back in the helicopter we flew southwest several miles over steep valleys and peaks to my second target, a mountain of weathered rock known as Jumbo Dome. In the helicopter, this trip took only minutes. When I returned on foot, I knew it would take days.

Near the top of Jumbo Dome, I dropped off the second food cache and cracked open some rocks. Chipping away the weathered brown rinds, they all looked the same inside—a dull pink array of medium crystals in random patterns. This told me the rocks had cooled underground, in place, without any movement or flow. With their distinctive coloring, it would be easy to map their extent. *Just follow the pink.*

We squeezed back into the chopper and flew to my last site, the creamy white top of Sugar Loaf Mountain. Walking on the rubble here made a hollow, crunching sound caused by hundreds of tiny air pockets in each stone. Inside the rocks, the matrix looked frothy. These rocks had cooled in gas at the surface. It would have been a deadly explosion.

Between the air pockets there were tiny crystal needles all pointing the same way. This told me which way this part had flowed. The edge of this rock field, more than a mile away, would be easy to spot against the grey landscape. When I came back and measured it all, I could find the center of the eruption by mapping where the flow directions met.

I left the third barrel there and said goodbye to my rocks. As I flew back to town, my head swam with everything I had seen and what it meant. The three rock types were different, but they still might have been formed by the same source of heat. Even with different surface expressions, they might be related—step-sisters with the same roving father deep underground.

This preview had shown me what I was up against, and a hint of the work ahead. I didn't yet know their full stories, but I was sure of one thing. It would take a force of nature to keep me from coming back.

11.

⁓ Starving Gary ⁓

 RAGGING ENOUGH GEAR FOR SIX WEEKS, I left the Sandvik House
to join the field camp crew gathering on campus. Field camp was like
boot camp for mappers. There were fifteen of us, all studying aspects
of geology or mining. The geologists among us welcomed the training.
This was hands-on practice in our intended careers, and we were
ready to be whipped into shape. But the mining engineers resented
it. Squeezing minerals from dirt requires a different set of skills than
mapping rock units. The mining students didn't believe they needed
this training and complained every step of the way.

Our leader was Dr. John Simms, a new member of the faculty
who had worked in the mines of South Africa and brought an air of
distinguished old-world experience. Our cook was Kathy Goff, a long-
time Alaskan who had been married five times. With her mane of black
curls, hearty laugh and a rifle under her pillow *just in case*, there was no
end to her stories, or her ex-boyfriends.

We piled into our bus, an ugly beast that was spray-painted black
and had a rack of caribou antlers mounted above the windshield. We
dubbed it the "tundrasaurus." With its bald tires spinning as it coughed
gray exhaust, we headed south to the Healy coal fields for a few days
of introductory mapping. Healy wasn't too far from my Sugar Loaf
Mountain. Dr. Simms gave me a few days off from measuring coal
seams so that I could hike up to my rocks. Two volunteers came with
me. This would be my first expedition.

From the highway, we saw the white mountain looking like a lump
of lopsided bread dough. On the map, the distance was only five miles
(8 km)—if we could fly. It was at least twice as long scrambling over the
hills. We would have just enough time to get to the base of the mountain,
where I could see how the white rocks had punched up from below.

I packed some food and we set off. It was a miserable hike, mostly uphill. After two days of steady climbing we arrived at the white base of Sugar Loaf around 10 p.m. With the sunlight still bright enough to read by, I went to work right away, measuring angles and collecting samples while my two helpers prepared our camp.

One volunteer set up the tent while the other, a mining engineering student named Gary Sherman, cooked our dinner. Gary, a burly guy, was so hungry after our climb that he used all the beans and every bit of our rice. By the time I realized that he had cooked *all* of our food, it had been eaten. I hadn't anticipated how much these fellows could eat. All that remained was a small bag of flour.

The next morning, I tried making pancakes on our little propane gas stove. But with no butter or shortening, all I could manage was a mushy flower paste with a charcoal crust—nothing like a pancake. We tried to eat the sticky burned batter but couldn't keep it down.

It would take two days to get back to Healy, passing through the same rough country we had hiked on the way up, but with no food. That night, Gary dreamed about hamburgers. They danced before him, with pickles and fine sauces, floating just out of his reach. After we set off in the morning, his dreams turned into hallucinations, tempting and taunting him with the promise of food.

He chased after his visions through patches of thick brush. We raced to keep up, abandoning all caution as the thickets and rocks scratched and scraped our skin.

I was so happy to see that ugly bus when we got back to the coal pit at Healy. After we had eaten, Gary told everyone how I had almost starved him. It was true. I hadn't brought nearly enough food. Next time I would budget for more.

～

From Healy we headed north. Four hundred miles later (640 km) we crossed the spine of the Brooks Range at Atigun Pass, at 4,739 feet (1,444 meters) above sea level, not far from where I had found the brachiopods the summer before.

We continued down the north side of the range to the North Slope, a sea of red tundra and reindeer moss. We had the road all to ourselves, and decided to take it all the way to the end and see what the north edge of the earth looked like. Seventy miles later (112 km), we got our wish.

About a quarter-mile past the Prudhoe Bay pipeline pump station, the gravel road ended unceremoniously at the Arctic Ocean, where choppy waves lapped against the gravel shore. There were no crashing waves or pounding surf, and we were disappointed. After all, this was the northern edge of the continental land mass of North America. From here there was nothing but water and ice all the way to the North Pole. Where was the drama we expected? We found it when we opened the door of the bus and the wind pelted us, then turned into a sudden snowstorm with gusts blowing sideways in a horizontal barrage of sleet. This wasn't unusual weather up here, even thought it was the height of the summer, the Fourth of July.

Climbing back into our bus, we drove south (the only direction possible) to the Prudhoe Bay oilfields. It was less windy away from the shore. We toured the Prudhoe Bay pump station, a handful of square buildings connected by enclosed wooden walkways. We were told that before the walkways were built, someone had been blown away into the sea.

At the pump station, crews lived in dorm-style quarters, rotating in and out every two weeks. With space a premium, they used a "hot-bunk" system, each bed assigned not to a particular person, but to a job. When your two weeks were up and you left, the person replacing you would inhabit your living space and take over your bed. Sharing quarters so intimately with someone you didn't know required keeping things tidy. One fellow showed us a picture frame in his room with his wife's smiling face. Then he flipped the frame around, and on the other side was a photo of his replacement's wife.

Our guide rattled off a well-rehearsed litany of the technological marvels of the pump station. By far, the most memorable stop on the tour was the cafeteria, which was loaded with trays of pastries, machines dispensing free candy bars, and packets of hot chocolate—as if sugar could make up for all the things they didn't have up here at the end of the world. We certainly agreed that it could. After days of eating canned camp food, we pounced on the desert racks, slipping doughnuts into our pockets as the guide smiled with indulgence and pretended not to notice.

Then we piled back into our bus and drove back over the Brooks Range, stopping near Galbraith Lake, where we set up our base camp near the road.

At first, we mapped the ground around us. Later, we were to break into smaller groups of three or four, moving farther out to set up remote "spike" camps, carrying with us tents, sleeping bags, and food for a few days. It was time to choose the teams.

The mining engineers clustered into one group. They made it clear they didn't want to walk very far.

The next group, dubbed the Bonzo Boys for their gung-ho attitude, boasted that they would cover as much ground as possible. That sounded good to me. I needed the training. After my experience starving Gary Sherman, I knew the gaps in my field knowledge were huge. But the Bonzo Boys wouldn't let me join them. They had taken a pact—no drugs, no booze, no women. Apparently, I was a vice.

As the next team formed, the pattern repeated—no girls allowed. That left me, Yvonne Grace, and two others—the four female students in camp. I thought we would make a good team, but Dr. Simms wouldn't have it. He didn't like the way the guys shut us out, insisting that they shuffle their teams to include us. I ended up in a group with a pair of mining engineers and a rather dashing fellow named Rob who looked like Rhett Butler in field gear.

The next day, the four of us hiked about five miles (8 km) to the west and set up the two tents. Once we got out there, the mining engineers sat in their tent, rarely leaving it except to eat pancakes with maple syrup—*real* maple syrup imported from Vermont. This they brought instead of work gear; clearly, they weren't going anywhere. It was up to Rob and me to cover the ground.

We made sweeps of the area, hiking farther from our little spike camp each day. On the third day, as we crossed a wide valley to map the rocks on the other side, it started to rain.I put on my rubberized rain jacket and pants, but Rob didn't bother.

"Are you sure you don't need it?" I asked.

"It's just a little shower," he said, not willing to take advice from a girl. It was a warm day and he was confident he could handle a little rain.

Before long the shower turned into a steady downpour. By then Rob was soaked, and it was too late for rain gear. Then the temperature dropped (this *was* the arctic) and the rain turned to sleet. Rob's wet clothes turned into ice—I could hear his jeans crackling and crunching against his knees with every step.

Hypothermia was not far behind.

We were six miles (9 km) from our pup tent when Rob stopped in the middle of the tundra, confused.

"Where's my blanket?" he said.

We were in the arctic wilderness, miles from anywhere—no trees, no people, and definitely no blanket.

"I want my blanket," said Rob. Then he fell to his knees and started rooting around in the tundra. "I know it's here somewhere."

He had lost touch with reality. This was worse than Gary Sherman's hamburger delusions because it takes days or weeks to die of starvation. I knew from my list of hazards that Rob's disorientation, caused by a drop in body temperature, was an advanced and dangerous stage of hypothermia.

Then Rob collapsed on the ground and curled up in a little ball. "I'll find it later," he said. "I'm going to sleep."

This is what I had feared; his body was shutting down.

"No, Rob," I said. "You have to get up."

"I'm too tired. Wake me up later."

I knew that if Rob fell asleep, there would be no "later" for him.

I had no radio, no way to get help. How do you force a stubborn man, insane from the cold, to walk for hours over uneven ground? How do you get him to safety when there's no safety to be found for miles, and all he wants is to curl up and die?

I told him his blanket was just beyond the next rock, and then the one after that. I tugged and I pulled and pushed and lied my way across six miles (10 km) of tundra, fighting him every inch of the way back to our dry little pup tent.

Once he was wrapped inside his down sleeping bag, I fired up our tiny cook stove and made him hot soup. It was an hour before he stopped shaking. When the blue in his lips turned pink again I knew the crisis was over. Rob wouldn't be joining Mister Franklin of Franklin Bluffs as a memorial name on the map after all.

The next morning the arctic sun was bright and glorious. But Rob was finished with spike camp. The four of us packed up our tents and headed back to base camp. Once there, Rob planted himself along with the mining engineers, refusing to leave sight of the bus. They didn't have to. They already had done enough mapping to pass the course.

By this time, five weeks into the course with only one more week to go, several of the geology students had come back, too, and were listlessly sitting around the camp eating big bowls of powdered mashed potatoes or whatever Kathy Goff cooked up, biding their time. There wasn't much else to do. The only entertainment we had the entire month and a half, except for a quick peek at a newspaper at Prudhoe Bay, was a book someone had brought—Peter Freuchen's *Famous Book of the Eskimos*. We divided it into pieces and swapped it around, reading about early Eskimo village life, with stories about wife-sharing and a local character the villagers didn't want near their dogs because his prized possession was a tin can that he used for boiling newborn puppies into stew.

I couldn't blame my fellow students for wanting to be finished with field work. But I needed to be out in the field, charging across the tundra, getting all the experience I could. What I learned out here would be vital for my thesis work later that summer. I would have no safety net, nothing to rely on except the experience I acquired out here.

It was time to join a new group. But only one team was still trudging through the tundra to map the rocks, and the team was full until Gary sprained his ankle. Then I took his place with the die-hards who wouldn't give up no matter what the arctic threw at them. This group didn't come here to eat pancakes. This group was here to work.

So I ended up in the "girl group" after all.

12.

Sold for a Steak

*T*HE LAST SPIKE CAMP GROUP INCLUDED ME, Yvonne Grace, and Laurel Burns who, after graduating, would go on to Stanford University to earn a doctorate in geophysics. In a male-dominated field that demanded physical endurance, we had to be tougher, smarter, and willing to work twice as hard.

The fourth member of our group was Joe Head, the drawling cowboy from Tom's Comco group. The four of us hiked off to set up another spike camp, this one even farther away, on the far edge of the mapping zone. To get there, we walked south on the Haul Road for about seven miles (11 km) before heading up into the hills another five miles (8 km).

From our spike camp, we covered the ground around us, sampling the rocks, determining rock type, and plotting the units on our map. When our food started to run out four days later, it was time to go back. It would be a long day's hike back to base camp, so we woke up early. After a good breakfast, we got dressed and took down the tents.

Yvonne didn't bother changing her clothes. She had quit wearing her jeans and shirts and now wore nothing but her two-piece long johns with their waffle-weave cotton that had once been white but were now a mottled gray. Even worse, the stretch in the bottoms had gone, and the crotch sagged down to her knees.

The rest of us folded our gear as we tucked it away in our backpacks. Yvonne had her own way of doing this, too. She shoved her things in haphazardly, not the most efficient use of space, and whatever didn't fit in the pack was tied to the outside. As we marched off across the slope, Yvonne's cooking pans, rain boots, and sleeping bag dragged behind her, flapping and jangling every step of the way.

After a few hours, we crested a hill and saw the pipeline and Haul Road stretching from the north horizon to the south. A cloud of dust in the distance was snaking toward us. It was a truck! If we could catch a ride, we would save seven miles (11 km) of hiking.

We ran down the slope as fast as we could, shouting and waving our arms to get the driver's attention. In this desolate landscape, he probably had never seen people running down from these hills. Curious, he eased his truck to a stop. Joe got to him first. When Laurel and I caught up, Joe and the driver were leaning against the cab, having a friendly chat about the driver's lonely job of delivering groceries to Prudhoe Bay.

"Thanks," said Joe. "We really appreciate you stopping to give me and my buddies a lift."

The trucker smiled and then looked over at us. When he realized that two of Joe's "buddies" were women, he gave Joe an odd stare. Then, Yvonne caught up with us in her stained droopy drawers, with her gear trailing behind her. The truck driver's jaw dropped.

Seeing the driver smoking was too much for Yvonne, who had not had a cigarette in two weeks. She yanked the cigarette from his mouth and began sucking on it furiously.

"I'm sorry, I'm sorry," she said, unable to stop herself.

Without invitation, Yvonne shed her backpack and crawled into the cab, riffling through the glove compartment until she found the rest of the pack. She ripped it open and stuffed two more cigarettes into her mouth.

"I'll pay you back," she said between drags. "I'll get you a pack. Yes, I'll buy you a whole carton. Then I'll quit tomorrow, and never smoke again. This is a bad habit. Bad, bad, Yvonne! I promise I'll never attack your cigarettes again. I'm really sorry about this. You . . . you don't have another pack, do you?"

The astonished trucker looked at Joe and the rest of us. In the thickest Texas drawl I'd ever heard, he asked, "What-all did you say you was a-doing out there in the tundra?"

We squeezed into the cab and Joe waxed poetic about the fold structures we found that had never been measured. The trucker nodded politely while we luxuriated in the scenery racing by, extra wonderful because we didn't have to walk it.

With Joe pointing the way, the driver pulled his big semi right up into our base camp, past the cluster of green tents, and stopped next to the bus.

Before he headed off, the trucker called Joe over to his window, and the two men chatted for a while. As Joe waved goodbye, I turned to him. "What did he want?"

Joe shrugged. "He wanted me to trade one of you girls for a steak."

"Come on, Joe. What did he really say?"

"Like I said, one of you ladies for a steak. I told him you weren't for sale."

"You mean he wanted to *buy* us?" Laurel asked. "With meat?"

"Not just any meat," said Joe. "Prime rib. But he didn't actually want to buy you. He said a loan would be fine."

Yvonne cocked her head. "Which one?"

"He didn't say," said Joe. "I guess any one of you would have worked."

At that point, I knew it had to be a preposterous joke. Trust Joe to come up with something so absurd.

Three days later, as we were inking the last bits of data onto the map, a cloud of dust blew up from the south. The Texan was back. Joe went out to meet him and came back with two big steaks wrapped in a white package.

Joe's crazy story was true after all.

"He thought it was worth a try," said Joe. "But when I told him you girls still weren't for sale, he said I might as well have these anyway—no hard feelings."

Kathy the cook divided one steak among fifteen of us. It was the only real meat we'd had in weeks. The other steak went entirely to Joe. He smiled as he attacked his fine meal, fit for a king, while the rest of us looked on like hungry dogs.

I didn't begrudge Joe his meal. He deserved every bite of it because good old Joe hadn't sold us after all. Not even for prime rib.

13.

❧ Who Stole My Weasel? ❧

$\mathscr{T}$HE BIG BLACK TUNDRASAURUS ROLLED into Fairbanks and we piled out. We had mapped a piece of the Brooks Range, and field camp was officially over. The joy of returning to civilization with its fresh food and clean clothes was overwhelming—until I remembered that I didn't have a place to live. Yvonne allowed me to pitch a pup tent in front of her place on College Road. She lived in a shack that represented the worst of both worlds—a cabin with no plumbing or central heat, but with all the road noise and car fumes from a busy street.

I didn't plan to camp at Yvonne's for long. In a few days I would head for the Alaska Range, this time without a group. But I wouldn't be alone. It's not wise to go into the wilderness by yourself, so we were encouraged to hire an assistant. In lieu of payment, the assistant would work for the experience. My friends all had summer jobs, so I had to look farther afield for an assistant.

My brother Ed, who had just finished high school, agreed to fly up and work for me. It would be his first major trip away from home.

I couldn't wait for his arrival. I had always been close to my "little" brother, who was seven years younger than I but now stood nearly a head taller. Laurel Burns drove me out to the airport to get him. As his plane landed, I recalled another time that I had waited for him to arrive.

Fifteen years before, my parents, after having three girls, decided to adopt a baby boy from Korea. As a child, I spent many mornings staring over my breakfast cereal at his photograph on the table, wondering when my new brother could come home. In 1963, after two years of waiting, little Ed was put on a seventeen-hour flight from Seoul to New York. On board were American soldiers and nurses and adopted children on their way to new homes. The airplane didn't have enough seats for all the passengers, so Ed offered to hold a baby on his lap and took care of the infant the entire trip. Ed was three at the time.

Now he was eighteen, and I was thrilled I could share my world in the north with him.

We spent a few days in town so I could brief him and make sure he had the right gear. Out in the field we would need sleeping bags, a tent, a cook stove, pans and dishes, maps, measuring equipment, sample bags, food for the hike in, raingear, down jackets, and clothes for six weeks. Every bit of this would be carried in on our backs. Seeing this sprawling pile of gear was Ed's first indication of what he was in for.

We loaded it all into our monstrous packs and got a ride south with Paul Metz, a professor from the Mineral Industry Research Lab. About a hundred miles (160 km) down the Parks Highway, we were dropped off at the town of Ferry, with a population of about thirty and a roadhouse that was closed in the winter, fall, and spring. This was as close to Buzzard Creek as the road would take us. A dirt path extended another six miles (9 km), but it was on the other side of the Nenana River. The ferry service that gave the town its name had been gone for decades and now the only way to get across the river was over a long railroad bridge that spanned 482 feet (147 m).

We stopped at the roadhouse for hamburgers. When the cook learned that we intended to cross the railroad bridge, he shook his head. He explained that the trains were frequent and fast, traveling up to 70 mph. If you met one on the long stretch of the bridge, you would be forced to jump over the edge and into the river. As we ate, he took great pleasure in telling us stories of crossings gone wrong, including the tale of two hippies who had tried to cross the railroad bridge in their yellow pickup truck. The pair had waited until right after a train crossed, assuming there wouldn't be another one for a while. But half-way across, a second train came at them, forcing them to drive off the bridge into the swift-moving water twenty-five feet (7.6 m) below. He didn't explain how the story ended, and I didn't stick around to ask.

We still had to cross the Nenana, one of the major tributaries of the Tanana River, and that railroad bridge was the only way. I stood at the edge and leaned down, putting my ear to the rail to feel for vibrations.

Nothing. I was betting our lives on this crossing. I would never forgive myself if something happened to my brother.

I signaled to Ed. With our bulky fifty- to sixty-pound packs weighing us down, we stepped onto the bridge. Between the cross ties, we could see angry swirls of brown water far below. Balancing on the boards, we walked with great caution to the bridge's mid-point. From there we ran to the other side as fast as we could. We made it with twenty minutes to spare before the next train thundered by. I was glad that we hadn't stayed at the roadhouse a little longer for pie.

I had always loved trains, and had never before seen them as a threat. That night I thought about all the ways Alaska continued to surprise me as we camped in the only shelter around, an abandoned caboose.

In the morning, we set off on foot heading down a muddy trail. Six miles (9 km) in, the trail ended at an unlocked cabin with a sign from the owners out front: "Please feel free to use this cabin. Just don't abuse it. Thank you."

Ed wanted to check it out. I wanted to keep moving. Without a trail, our hiking was about to get tougher. We still had several more miles to go up and over the mountains and had no time to waste.

Ed was disappointed. He had flown all the way from New York to help me. We would have plenty of nights stuck in a tent. Couldn't we spend just one night in this friendly cabin?

Okay, I said. Just for one night.

We settled in, dry and warm with the welcome comforts of a woodstove to cook our bean soup and a rodent-chewed mattress to park our sleeping bags on.

After breakfast the next morning, Ed sat on the porch and polished his rifle, a heavy bolt-action .30-.06 moose-hunting gun. Dr. Turner had lent it to us. I didn't want to bring it along because we already had Sally. With the weight of our gear, and the rocks we would bring back, one big gun was enough. But Ed insisted on bringing that rifle, as if he didn't trust my shooting, and he toted that thing everywhere. I was learning that my adorable baby brother could be stubborn and didn't always appreciate that his sister was the boss.

As I was washing our dishes, I heard a mechanical whine coming from the west. There was no trail from that direction, let alone a road. I went out to listen and could hardly believe it when a Toyota Landcruiser as blue as a robin's egg emerged from the brush, grinding its gears as it lurched through the tundra. A man walked beside it, his clothes stained with grease. A pistol was tucked into his belt.

"Who stole my weasel?" he growled.

Did he own the cabin? His tone didn't match the friendly note on the door.

"Who stole my weasel?" he repeated, shouting this time.

Ed came out of the cabin with the rifle tucked under his arm. Seeing Ed's rifle, the man whipped out his pistol. As he did, four more men tumbled out of the Landcruiser, guns drawn and aimed at us.

A Wild West shootout was *so* not on my list.

"Ed," I said in my firmest big-sister voice. "Put down your *bear* gun *right now* and come meet these nice gentlemen."

He put the rifle down on the porch, and the visitors lowered their guns.

The men explained that they were hunters who came into the area every year to shoot moose, carrying their kills back out to the highway in a type of tracked vehicle called a weasel. They parked it in the same spot every year, but this year it was gone. Someone had driven off in it. They were following the tracks, which led past the cabin.

I explained that we had not stolen their vehicle. I showed them my equipment: rock hammer, field lens, and the cylindrical magnetometer that looked like R2-D2's robot son. These instruments, I explained, were hardly the tools of a thieving joy-rider. Then I pointed out that the missing weasel's tracks in the dirt were old and eroded. Whoever stole it had driven it away before the last rain.

They agreed with my logic, cooled down, and we had a chat about getting around in the bush. I complimented them on their Landcruiser, and they showed me the secret to its off-road success—a driveshaft that was twice as sturdy as any other model of truck. I wished them well as they squeezed back into their vehicle and drove off to find their weasel. Then I breathed a sigh of relief. I didn't ever again want to find myself staring down the barrel of an angry man's gun.

We hadn't even arrived at my first set of rocks, but already we had faced two life-threatening situations. I hoped that we had used up our quota of danger, although somehow that seemed unlikely.

14.

Field Theory of Relativity

WE LOADED OUR PACKS AND SET OFF for Buzzard Creek. It was a steep uphill climb all the way and the straps on our backpacks dug into our skin.

I checked the map often since the mountains ahead all looked the same. It would be easy to get lost.

After a few hours we had made pitifully small progress and faced a choice: We could skirt the mountains and take the easier long way around. Or we could head over the top and cut out miles of hiking. I decided to go up and over. It looked like such a short distance on the map.

This wasn't my wisest decision. This mountain was a bastard, getting steeper with every step as it fought us, throwing rocks down on us from above. We still couldn't see our target, and the sun was sinking.

Then, miraculously, the ground leveled off. We had made it to the top. From here, I could look down on the ponds of the maar pits, carved into the flank of the next mountain over. We had climbed the wrong mountain.

We hiked down the slope, crossed a stream gully, and climbed back up the next mountain. With our destination in sight, I could watch the maar pits getting closer with each step and the distance didn't seem to matter.

As we angled up, I saw piles of bear droppings. We had seen these before, but here they were fresh; a bear was nearby. This was a powerful reminder to keep up our guard.

Finally we got to the lip of the craters, exhausted and sore. There would be no mapping that day. It would take the last of our energy to set up camp.

I found the food barrel where I had left it, with the cache intact.

We pitched the tent on the lip of the crater rim, enjoying the view.

To our backs were the mountains. To the north, the slope continued down into the Tanana River flats more than a hundred miles away, with no sign of civilization in any direction. I wondered how many people had slept on this crater rim, waking each day to this view. Maybe no one, ever. This was a sobering thought.

Ed cooked a fine meal of spaghetti and protein kibbles while I roughed out a schedule for the days ahead.

I was finally here, about to study these rocks as they'd never been studied before. Could I make these rocks tell their secrets? And if they did, would I be clever enough to hear them? I wondered what I would learn about these rocks and what they would reveal about me.

It wasn't long before we discovered our campsite was no paradise. We were exposed to gales of wind that swept down the mountain flanks, and had to walk half a mile to Buzzard Creek for water unless we were willing to drink stagnant brown pond slime squirming with mosquito larvae. Still, with the crater rim underfoot, my work progressed on schedule the first week as I spent nearly every daylight hour (and there were many) focused on the rocks. Ed didn't mind cooking since that meant eating; I was too engaged in the work to be dealing with food. Although we didn't have much variety in our dry ingredients, Ed was able to combine them in interesting ways.

He found fresh blueberries in the springy marshes that he mashed into a sauce for the spaghetti with protein nuggets. This became our favorite meal and was often the highlight of the day. Ed thought he had invented a new culinary treat. I tried to tell him that although this dish was pretty great out here, back in the real world it probably wouldn't taste very good. He didn't believe me. He didn't yet understand that out in the field, perception is different. Food tastes better. Jokes seem funnier. Away from civilization, any enjoyment is magnified a dozen times.

I had discovered this at field camp. The phenomenon affected people, too. Away from civilization, you bond with people in a field crew in a special way. It was easier to see their good side and overlook their bad. In a crew where everyone works together, the people around you become your best friends.

However, once you got back to town, your view of that field friend invariably reverted to whatever it was before. You might remember that you never liked them in the first place, or were indifferent as you realized that it was just lack of choice that made you appreciate their meager few good points in the field.

Everyone who worked in the bush experienced what I came to think of as my own theory of relativity—"Alaskan field relativity." This wasn't about physics, it was based on perception. According to what I had seen, it seemed to me that a person's appreciation of things (a meal, a friend, or a joke) was magnified in direct proportion to how long they had been in the field. This effect was completely reversible upon returning to town.

I saw this effect demonstrated over and over. No one was immune. If you didn't understand that your perception had changed, you might do something you would regret later. I saw a sad example of this when I visited a camp where the pilot liked to tell jokes. I was fresh from town and didn't think his jokes were funny. But his crew had been out in the bush for weeks and thought he was a scream. "Tell us some more," they urged, and then fell over each other in hysterics when his punch-line ended in yet another duck imitation.

By the end of the summer, the pilot became convinced that he had real comic talent. That fall, he quit his job flying helicopters and took his act to Las Vegas, where it flopped miserably. By the time he accepted the fact that he wasn't funny, his pilot's license had expired and he couldn't find work. The last I heard of him, he had been caught stealing packaged meat from a grocery store.

Alaska had that effect on people. It was a big place that bred big dreams. But when they shattered, they left a big mess. I did not want my dreams to end up that way.

Into our second week at Buzzard Creek, Ed's enthusiasm started to drag. It became a challenge to get him to do anything but cook. He lost our only knife. Then he lost his glasses and couldn't see. That meant when I combed the hills to collect samples, I would have no help carrying the rock samples back to camp.

It was clear Ed didn't want to be here. I had warned him that field work would be different than the camping he was used to. In upstate

New York, camping involves a vacation next to a road with a car full of gear and a store down the street. That kind of "wilderness" isn't particularly wild.

It is difficult to explain that feeling of isolation being completely removed from civilization, with nothing between you and the furies of arctic nature except a millimeter of tent fabric. Here we relied on our legs and our wits, with nothing more than what we could carry on our backs.

Field exploration is bone-weary work. You can expect to be sore, exhausted, hungry, wet, cold, or too hot most of the time. The discomfort is relentless. After twelve to eighteen hours of work, you don't have a dry home to collapse in; instead, you get yourself some dehydrated food soaked in stream water, then you crawl into your soggy tent and sleep in your dirty clothes, hoping that your sores will heal enough overnight so you don't have to start the next day already in pain.

By the end of the third week, my work at Buzzard Creek was finished. Ed was all done, too. There was no point trying to coax him into hiking up to Jumbo Dome. By then, having him around was worse than being alone. He wasn't complaining openly, but his silent misery was sapping my energy. I had to get him back to the real world.

We packed up our camp and left the stony rim of the maars where we had lived for the better part of a month. This time, we went the long way around the mountains. Two days later, we made it to the highway and hitch-hiked to Fairbanks. Usually it was a joy to return to town. This time, I came back in defeat because so much work was left undone and the summer was melting away.

In Fairbanks, I pitched our pup tent in the weeds next to Yvonne's cabin and thought about what to do next. Soon the tension between Ed and me erupted into a shouting match on the sidewalk along College Road. With our yelling and stomping, and insults hurled back and forth, we must have put on quite a spectacle for people driving by—a real live arctic soap opera. With his Korean features, Ed was sometimes mistaken for a Native American. Perhaps that added to the appeal of the "show" as people actually got out of their cars to hear what we were arguing about. When we saw the cameras come out, we came to our senses and took off running, tears running down our cheeks as we laughed so hard at those crazy tourists—and even harder at ourselves.

As suddenly as it started, the fight was over. Although Ed flunked out of Wilderness Camping 101, it wasn't his fault that he wasn't a field geologist at heart. Besides, how could I stay angry at the brother who the first year I was away at college had risen a half-hour early every morning to feed my horse?

It was time for Ed to go back to New York, a little wiser for having survived both the wilderness and dealing with his big sister as his boss.

And I had to get back to the field.

I scouted for a new assistant in the deserted halls of the Brooks Building, hoping to find someone who understood what they were getting into. Actually, I was so desperate that almost anyone would do.

I spotted my victim at the geology bulletin board reading the notices. Her name was Harriet, an undergraduate student with blonde curls spiraling out like a giant sunflower. I had seen her in the happy camper van on that first trip to the Brooks Range. I had wanted to meet her but she wasn't in any of my classes. She had just returned from a hiking trip to Katmai, the Valley of Ten Thousand Smokes, and was looking for another adventure to round out her summer. Boy, did I have a deal for her: room and board (tent and beans) and all the rocks she could carry.

Harriet signed on and we hitch-hiked south to Healy. From the highway, we hiked in to the top of Jumbo Dome, pitching our tent in a windy updraft with a view of the north flank of the range. When we mapped the dome in less than a week, I felt giddy with hope. With Harriet on board, I just might be able to knock off my thesis work after all.

With only one target left, we packed up camp and climbed down Jumbo Dome, then set off across the tundra toward the ivory-colored slopes of Sugar Loaf Mountain. A few hours along, we came to a little creek, maybe twelve feet across. I couldn't see the bottom but it didn't look too deep. I had crossed tributaries all summer with no trouble, and some had looked worse than this one.

I started to head across.

"Wait!" said Harriet, pulling a ball of nylon twine out of her pack.

"Tie this rope on you first."

"You've got to be kidding," I said. "That's not a rope; it's a clothes-line."

"It's always a good idea to tie onto something when you're crossing a river."

"River?" I said. "This is just a creek, not even big enough to have a name. Do you really think this stream is going to be a problem?"

"Probably not," she said, "but tie it on anyway, just to be safe."

I felt silly, but tied the clothes-line around my belt. Then, as Harriet held onto the other end, I waded in. Five steps in, the water rushed over the top of my rubber boots, then up to my thigh. The current sucked my feet out from under me and I fell face down into the water, my pack pushing me down.

I was a swimmer. Back in college I had trained as a lifeguard and had been captain of the synchronized swimming team. But none of this did me any good here. In the icy cold water, my body was instantly paralyzed. With my head under the water, I couldn't lift it up to breathe. I couldn't do anything.

But Harriet could. She pulled on her little rope and dragged me back to the shore, sputtering and coughing, barely able to comprehend what had just happened.

I had crossed this same creek earlier in the summer with Gary Sherman. It was no problem then. But now in late August, it was choked with snow melt washing down from the upper reaches. It didn't look deeper or swifter, but it was.

I would not have believed I could drown in a little stream like this, but now I knew better. Without Harriet and her little rope, I wouldn't have stood a chance. I would never underestimate a creek like this again.

But we still had to cross it.

We hiked along the creek, looking for a better place to get across. Walking was harder for me now that I was weighted down with a pack full of wet gear. My clothes were sopping; I was losing body heat with every step.

We came to a spot that Harriet thought looked better. This time, she waded in while I stood on the shore and held the string-rope tied onto her. She was swept under, too, and it was my turn to pull her out like a flounder. Now all of our gear was soaked.

We made our way downstream like a pair of zombies, our legs stiff, our clothes clinging to us like glue. Every step took us farther in the wrong direction, adding more distance to our hike, and still we were no closer to crossing that creek.

Then the creek widened. My eyes saw more brown water and warned me that this would be even more treacherous, but my mind didn't agree. If the stream was wider, then the bottom couldn't be as deep, right?

"I'm going to try it here," I said to Harriet. "Tie me on."

She looped her line around my belt and I waded in. A third of the way across, I was still standing. So far, so good. Then I got to the middle. The water was over my knees and a strong current threatened to pull me in. But it didn't. I kept moving forward. Then I was past the middle. Now the water was just at my knees, and then lower. Several steps later, I made it to the other side!

I untied the rope, wound it into a ball, and tossed it across the creek to Harriet. She tied one end onto her belt, then attached the loose end to a stick and threw it back to me. I anchored her from my side. As she went in, a cold shadow fell on my shoulders. It was still afternoon, but in this draw the sun had ducked behind the hills and the temperature dropped with it. This was not good. We couldn't afford to get any colder.

Harriet, two inches shorter than I, was struggling.

"You've got it," I shouted. "Almost half-way there."

She made it across, but she was shaking—not shivering, but uncontrollably shaking—a clear sign of hypothermia. I was feeling it, too. We were still miles from Sugar Loaf Mountain, but there was no more hiking in us that day.

Our reserves were spent; our bodies couldn't take any more. Every part of us had been soaked in ice water; everything we carried had been dunked. We couldn't ignore that our bodies were going into shock. We needed warmth and rest.

"Let's camp right here," I said, dropping my pack on the stream bank. Harriet's cheeks flushed rose-pink with relief.

So we pitched the tent and changed out of our thoroughly drenched clothes and into the merely damp ones from the bottom of the packs.

While Harriet fired up the tiny bottle stove to make instant soup, I examined old Sally. The inside of the barrel was wet. It would rust if it was not cleaned. That shotgun was our lifeline, as vital to our survival as Harriet's rope had been. From the piles of bear sign along the bank I knew the bears fished in this creek. Normally we wouldn't have camped so close to one of their favorite stomping grounds, but we were in no shape to hike any farther.

There was solvent and gun oil in the big food barrel up on Sugar Loaf Mountain, but none here with us. So I rubbed old Sally down with the only cleaner I had, a squeeze of Dr. Bonner's all-purpose mint oil soap. That soap was amazing. We used it to wash everything—our dishes, our clothes, even our hair if we felt like dunking our heads in a stream.

For the first time that day, something went right—I discovered that along with its many other uses, this all-purpose mint oil soap both cleaned *and* oiled shotgun barrels. With good old Sally all clean and shiny, I brushed my teeth with that soap, too, right there in that nameless bear-splatter creek.

I hoped the bears didn't like our minty perfume.

⁓

The next morning, after hours of luxurious sleep, we woke up fully recharged and ready to roll. With no bears in sight, we packed up camp and set off. By noon, we were at the base of the mountain. It wasn't hard to find where Sugar Loaf erupted from the ground. It was where the rock rubble changed from dark gray to puce white.

We climbed up to its flat-ridged peak and set up camp, our tent touching the clouds as we looked down on the valley below. From here we could see Denali rising from the horizon. The top, bare just weeks ago, was now dusted in snow. Winter was coming.

For the next several days, we hiked all over that mountain and the surrounding ridge. One morning as we prepared our packs for the day, our tent was caught in a gust of air and blew away like a triangular balloon. We chased it halfway down the mountain. After that, we camped farther down, nestled in shrub.

At the end of two weeks, we had mapped it all. The samples I needed, a few hundred pounds of rock, were bagged and tagged and ready for the lab. We had done it! We had beaten the snow. It was time to go home.

I had arranged for a helicopter to retrieve us with all of our gear and rock samples. Helicopters were expensive, but I had included three precious hours of chopper time into my budget and was going to use every minute of it to get us home.

We packed our camp and waited for our ride at the appointed time. The wind blew up the mountain, cold and frosty.

We waited an hour, then another. Had something gone wrong? Had the helicopter company forgotten about us? Had the pilot lost the map I gave him marked with our pickup spot? Had he crashed?

We tried not to play "worst-case scenario," but it wasn't easy sitting there in the cold completely exposed, our tent packed away, every second a chilly reminder of the approaching winter.

There was no hiking out, not with hundreds of pounds of rock samples and that nameless creek to cross. So we waited up there on Sugar Loaf Mountain with no way to call anyone. For the first time that summer, I was completely dependent on somebody else. It wasn't a good feeling.

The longer we sat, the colder we got as the wind gusted around us. Just as we were setting the tent back up for shelter, I heard a low drone in the distance. "He's coming!" I said. "Quick, stuff the tent back in."

While Harriet shoved the tent back into the pack, I flagged the chopper down with a three-foot square signal panel of fluorescent pink plastic. The helicopter landed beside us. We hoisted our gear and samples into the back and strapped ourselves in.

As we flew across the rim of the Buzzard Creek Maars, I saw a tan grizzly bear, sniffing the ground where my tent had been. As we flew over it, the bear reared up and snarled at the helicopter. Even from up in the chopper, I could see his curved yellow teeth.

I said goodbye to the places I had known so intimately that summer, those rocks I had dreamed of and lived on. I would never walk among them again.

Then I looked ahead across the wide expanse of the Tanana River flats and finally to the Chena River looping around Fairbanks.

There'd be no more dry beans and rice coaxed into soup. No more wearing the same socks for a month. Now there would be clean showers and fresh sheets and a soft gentle bed to cradle my dreams.

Best of all, I could walk without having to carry forty pounds or more on my back.

It would be a massive job to analyze all those samples and sift through the volumes of field notes and measurements to piece together a story that would define me as a failure or a success as a "master of science." The data could take years to sort out, assuming I could do it. But that was a problem for another day.

For now, I was flying, in every sense of the word.

15.

✎ The Bog ✎

*E*UPHORIA IS SO FLEETING. In no time at all I was back to the grind, with classes and homework and a mound of rock samples that needed my attention. I learned how to cut rocks into paper-thin sections, shaving them down until they were so thin that I could see through them. Viewing these thin sections under a microscope, I could see inside the crystals, even the tiniest of grains.

As agreed, I went to work for Dr. Turner, my salary funded by his Department of Energy grant, compiling a huge geothermal map of the state. This was the first comprehensive geothermal map of Alaska. The drafting was painstaking work but I loved it, laying down delicate swirls and lines on the translucent master sheets as I translated reams of obscure data into a visual format, rendering it accessible and clear.

By this time I had spent five years living in dormitories and I felt it was time to move off-campus. Tom wasn't ready to leave so he stayed in the dorm. We were both in our early twenties and wondered if we were getting too serious, too young, and too fast. A little perspective might not be a bad thing.

I looked for housing near campus, but couldn't find anything. Everything had been rented, even old miners' cabins covered in sod, sprouting weeds from the roof, and sinking into the permafrost, like the hobbit house my friend Bruce Campbell rented that didn't quite allow him to stand up all the way. I would have to live farther from town. Forty minutes away in the Goldstream Valley, a group of friends lived in a ghetto of cheap cabins that we called "the bog." The cabins had no plumbing but the rent was low. I bought a beat-up Datsun with questionable brakes, loaded everything I owned into the back seat, and moved into my own little place in the bog.

From the outside, my little red cabin looked pleasantly rustic with a stand of birch trees in front and an outhouse off to the side. The cabin was built on a patch of half-melted permafrost and had tilted a few degrees to the back. The swamp behind it was a mosquito paradise when it wasn't frozen. Fortunately, that wasn't often.

Inside was a twelve-foot square room with plywood walls and a sleeping shelf in the back. It had a woodstove for heat. The "kitchen" was a wood bench with a small portable refrigerator-freezer, plugged into the cabin's only electrical outlet, and a bucket for water. For showers, we drove to campus and used the gym. It was very basic, but after spending the summer sharing a pup tent, having my own cabin seemed like a treat.

In mid-September, we bog-dwellers rented a flat-bed truck and some chain-saws to cut firewood from a forest-fire burn site. We spent all week working together cutting, splitting, and transporting the logs. By Friday night, our muscles ached from the strain, but it was good to see those tidy stacks of firewood outside our cabins, enough to get through the winter.

With some of the scrap logs, I built furniture for my cabin. My "chairs" were fat log stools. My table was a square of plywood nailed to four logs. It wasn't fancy, but it did the job.

As winter set in, I was so pleased with my snug little cabin that I threw a party. Tom brought his stereo system so we could have music. We unplugged the refrigerator to provide electricity for his stereo. I fried pizza on top of my woodstove and, with all of our friends crowded inside, it was a lively little crowd.

One of the guests noticed the tilt in the floor. Just for fun, he put a pencil down on the floor to see if it would roll. Sure enough, it scooted all the way to the back wall. This provided a great party game—pencil races.

I was eager to try another party trick. I had heard that if it was cold enough, you could throw a pan of hot water into the outside air and no water would reach the ground. I wasn't sure what was supposed to happen; would it turn into ice? The night was cold, about -30 F (-34 C), so we decided to give it a try. I heated up a skillet with a thin film of water, and we all trooped outside.

As I flung the water into the air, we all ducked, expecting droplets of hail to fall on us. But nothing came down; nothing at all. Instead, the hot water instantly vaporized into a little cloud of flash-fried steam and drifted away.

What a great way to christen my new home. When all the guests had left, I snuggled in, ready for winter.

At least I thought I was ready. But as the temperature dropped lower and lower, my cabin would not retain the heat. No matter how many fires I lit, it wouldn't stay warm. My friends in the other cabins could build fires that lasted until morning. At the end of the day, they would come back to a house that was cool but not frozen. But not mine.

No matter how many logs I fed the woodstove, it was always well below freezing in the cabin the next morning. When I returned from school at night, it was even colder. It got so bad I had to put the milk in the refrigerator (unplugged)—not to chill it but to keep it from freezing solid. Even inside the insulated fridge, the top of the milk iced over. When the inside of your freezer is the warmest place in your house, something is terribly wrong.

The cold wasn't just inconvenient; it affected every aspect of my life. Sleeping was difficult because I had to wake up every few hours during the night to feed the fire. Eating was impossible at home because everything was frozen. And forget about washing dishes or anything else.

My neighbors didn't understand it. They assumed I didn't know how to make a good fire.

"When you go to bed," they said, "turn down the damper."

"I am turning it down," I told them.

"Not far enough," they said.

One wickedly cold night, just before I went to bed, I loaded the woodstove with logs and cranked the damper as far down as I dared.

In the middle of the night, I woke up with my head pounding, my throat blocked. The cabin was full of smoke! When I opened the front door to air out the room, the thermometer read -40 F (-40 C). Feeling dizzy, I couldn't think of where to go; I couldn't think at all.

Exhausted and angry, I needed sleep badly. If I went to sleep in my cabin, the fumes might suffocate me. If I dragged my sleeping bag out to my car, I could freeze to death. Neither choice was appealing.

I propped the front door wide open and laid my sleeping bag on the floor. I figured there would be less smoke down there. Then I crawled into the bag and passed out.

In the morning I woke up on the cold floor. With the door left wide open, the smoke was gone, and it was a sinful -40 F (-40 C) inside. But my thoughts were now clear. The headache in the middle of the night had probably been an early symptom of carbon-monoxide poisoning. No wonder I hadn't been able to think straight. Going to sleep in a room full of smoke had been chancy. I was lucky to be alive.

I wasn't about to tempt fate again and refused to spend another night in that death trap. I loaded everything I owned into the back of my car and moved into a friend's place, where I slept on the floor.

After I left the bog, a PhD student rented my cabin, confident he could handle a woodstove better than I. Oddly enough, he had the same problem, unable to keep the little house warm no matter how much firewood he burned. In a fit of frustration, he peeled back the plywood wall. He was shocked to discover that there was no insulation behind it. The six-inch gap meant to insulate the wall was empty. Apparently, the slum landlord had tacked up the inner and outer walls of this cabin without a single scrap of foam or fiberglass or anything else.

My fire-making skills were vindicated but this gave me no satisfaction. Unable to focus on my studies, I came perilously close to flunking out. If I didn't pull my grades up, I would be finished.

Now I would have to work harder than ever.

16.

⊷ Duke Apartments ⊷

After Christmas, Tom and I realized we didn't want to live apart. After our crazy summer schedules and my bog cabin misadventure, we were still together, and decided to move into the same place. We found our love nest in the Duke Apartments on College road, a modest one-bedroom rental with heat, power, and hot water that didn't have to be chopped and boiled.

From "the Duke" we could walk to campus in half an hour. This was important because my poor old Datsun was making banging sounds and needed a new engine that would cost more than the car was worth.

It was sheer bliss to sleep all night without waking up to feed a fire, and the shower in the bathroom felt like my own magic fountain.

Freed from the stress of bog life survival, my grades perked up. My thesis research began yielding results, too, although not in the way I had hoped. As the samples came back from the lab, it became clear that my three rock formations were not related geologically after all. Their chemistry and ages didn't match up. The only feature young enough to be a possible source of heat turned out to be a cold dead end.

Although it was not the story I expected, it was still a story. Actually, it was three stories from three different ages. One of them confirmed some seismic work done by another graduate student. Combining our work made a strong case for the position and depth of the leading edge of the subduction zone that dipped under the Earth's crust.

I wrote about my findings in a five-page report for Holister Grant's scientific journal at the Alaska survey. I was proud when it was published. It was the most difficult thing I had ever written.

For the thesis, I would have to write twenty times that amount.

Still, the pieces were coming together. If I squeezed my eyes together just right, I could see a glimmer of light at the end of the tunnel. It gave me hope that I might conquer this degree after all. It was hard to believe that a farm girl like me, a teacher who couldn't get a job, could end up an explorer—a master of rocks.

With new confidence, I churned my way through the term, ready for the final exams in May. I wasn't too worried. I was prepared, anticipating every question they might ask.

But there was a question from Tom I did not see coming.

Tom was about to graduate in the spring of 1979 with his mining degree and his family was coming from New Jersey for commencement. One night as I studied for a stratigraphy exam, Tom suggested that since his family was already coming north, why not save his parents a second trip later by having the wedding at the same time as the graduation ceremonies?

"Wedding?" I asked. "Is this a proposal?"

It was. Although not the most romantic proposal, the point was made—you and me, forever. What did I think of that?

I thought yes. The times we spent apart never got in the way of the fact that we were perfect life partners—not perfect people, but perfectly matched. We both were self-starters, driven, and independent; we made an exceptional team. The time was right, and the guy was right. I couldn't imagine going through life with anyone else.

Tom suggested a ski chalet on the top of Ester Dome, just north of town, would be a great place for a wedding. The lodge was made of logs laid down in a hexagonal shape, with wrap-around views that looked down on all sides of the mountain. But no one skied there now. The lodge had been closed to the public because the government found that the ground water had too much arsenic. With its poisoned well water, Tom figured it wouldn't cost much to rent.

We tracked down the owner. We promised to bring in our own water, and agreed to clean up after ourselves and to return the key promptly. We slipped him some cash, including a refundable deposit, and scheduled the wedding for the day after Tom's graduation.

I didn't have time for much planning. With the semester winding down, I faced a big hurdle—the comprehensive exam. A requirement of the program, this was no ordinary test, it was an all-day ordeal. To demonstrate my competence, I would be questioned on every geologic specialty field. If I failed, I was out. I had seen this happen to too many friends and I knew that if my shortage of undergraduate geology courses was going to trip me up, this was where it would happen.

Everything was happening at once—my comprehensive exam, Tom's graduation, and the wedding all squeezed into a single long weekend, from Friday to Monday. A few days after the wedding, Tom was scheduled to fly off to his summer job north of Nome.

I was petrified by the make-or-break exam. Yet I wasn't worried about the wedding. After all, it was just a big party. What could go wrong?

My parents agreed to come up, along with my sister Christine, the former carnival queen. Christine would join Yvonne Grace as a bridesmaid. I bought long cotton wrap-around skirts (no fittings required) and sewed coordinating peasant blouses: yellow for Yvonne, and orange for my sister, and white for me, trimmed with lace from my grandmother's wedding dress.

For invitations, I drew a pen-and-ink winter scene on a sheet of paper that announced the details, and copied the page on a Xerox machine. We passed out these wedding flyers to our friends and professors and posted some on the Brooks Building walls.

For music, I recorded myself on a cassette recorder playing a piano. I had learned to play the piano as a kid, listening to my grandfather, who had been a honky-tonk player during the Depression.

Next was the food. I ordered a cake from the bakery downtown. The rest would be potluck—whatever people wanted to bring. This solved the problem of having to count heads. If everyone brought something, no matter how many people showed up, we would have the right amount of food.

Yvonne was appalled.

"Potluck?" she said. "What kind of wedding is this?"

"An easy one."

Yvonne shook her head. "At least let me coordinate the menu. I'll bring a ham and a roast. Now, what else shall I tell people to bring?"

"That's simple," I said. "Tell everyone to bring whatever they cook the best."

"Are you serious?"

I was. Why would I ask people to bring their *worst* dish? I didn't understand Yvonne's confusion as she walked away, shaking her head.

Yvonne was a true friend. She did what I asked, and invited people to bring their best food. As I had suggested, she asked *everyone,* including people she had never met. In the supermarkets and in the parking lots, wherever she went, she invited complete strangers to bring their best dish to my special day.

On the day of my comprehensive exam, I sat in a room on the top floor of the Brooks Building staring at a thick packet of questions, my mind gripped in a blizzard of fear. The clock on the wall ticked the seconds away; was it always this loud? I had six hours to finish this test, but I couldn't catch a single thought as the doubts swirled around me, my mind as blank as the empty pages I was supposed to fill.

I tried to read the questions but my eyes wouldn't focus. In my head, all the words on the pages said the same thing. *Answer me wrong and you can kiss your graduate degree goodbye.*

Finally, after long minutes of this, I recognized some words on the page, and then a few more. I pieced them together and realized that I understood the question. *And I knew the answer*!

My mind was like a zipper that had come unstuck. After answering that first question, I was able to pull apart another question, then another. Although I didn't exactly glide through the text, I was able to complete it with a great deal of snagging and tugging and backing up.

Six hours later, I flipped the test over, the signal that I was done. Immediately, Tom pounced into the room. I hadn't even noticed he had been waiting at the door.

"Hurry," he said. "We need to get downtown. We've got to apply for a marriage license and maybe get blood tests."

My mind was still in geology land. Did he just say someone wanted our blood?

"Come on!" he said. "The municipal building closes in fifteen minutes. If we don't make it, the wedding can't happen."

I had just taken the most brutal test of my life—the ink wasn't even dry—and already I was embroiled in the next crisis.

We raced downtown and got to the recorder's office just minutes before it closed. We filled out the forms—no blood test required—and dropped the papers into the wire basket on the file clerk's desk. With a big metal stamp, the clerk pounded the forms, imbedding the date. Then she checked her watch.

"Congratulations," she said. "You have made today's filing with ninety seconds to spare. You can collect your license on Monday morning."

Monday was the day of the wedding. We had made it by the skin of our teeth.

We had no time to celebrate or relax. Our apartment, a jumble of textbooks and study notes, needed a serious cleanup because our wedding guests were arriving the next morning.

It was time to meet the in-laws.

Our family gathered for this photo in 1974 just as I was thinking of heading north to Alaska. Earl and Eunice Ross, my dad and mom, are in front. In back, from left, are my brother Ed, my younger sister Stephanie, me, and my older sister Christine.

Tom and me on the University of Alaska Fairbanks campus in 1977.

$\mathcal{O}$ur field-camp crew stops for a photo at the Arctic Circle. I am seventh from the left. In front of me, from left, are Laurel Burns (sitting), Yvonne Grace (kneeling), and Kathy Goff (standing). Gary Sherman, behind Kathy, reads the sign. Joe Head is at the far left.

Tom pauses to inspect a crevasse on a climb in 1976.

Climbing Panorama Peak with spikes clamped onto my boots.

On one of our first dates, Tom and I climbed Panorama Peak. "If you fall here, you'll die," he told me. I was not happy.

*D*r. John Simms, facing the camera, and the dust-coated bus that took us over the Haul Road to the Brooks Range.

*T*his antler-decorated bus, which we called the "Tundrasaurus," took us on a geology field trip into the Arctic. That's our cook tent to the right.

*O*ur camp on a high ridge of Sugar Loaf Mountain. The white mountain behind me is Mount McKinley (Denali), already covered in snow. It was late August, and winter was on the way.

I'm standing on the volcanic
rim of the Buzzard Creek Marrs
overlooking the Tanana Flats.

My brother Ed sits on a food barrel surrounded by supplies as we prepare to set up camp on the slope of the Buzzard Creek Maars.

My house in the bog out in Goldstream Valley. It wasn't much bigger than my car.

I'm in full field gear attire. The packs weighed between forty and sixty pounds, without the rocks.

Full gear with my shotgun.

From left, Tom, me, Tom's mom, Rosemarie Helm, and Tom's younger sister, Andrea, at Tom's graduation.

Tom and me on top of Ester Dome at our wedding on May 9, 1979. I don't know where that dog came from.

This was taken the summer we got married.

17.

❧ Lords, Ladies and Strangers ❧

$\mathcal{I}$ HAD SEEN TOM'S FAMILY ONCE before on a brief visit to New Jersey. At the time, I was the girlfriend, not the future daughter-in-law. Tom was the first of his siblings to get married, and so was I. Together, we were charting new territory in our family dynamics.

We picked up Tom's mom, stepdad, and ten-year-old sister Andrea at the airport and drove them to the guest housing we had arranged for them at the university. Once they put down their bags, Tom's mother turned to me.

"All right," she said. "Now that the room is taken care of, let's see your rings."

Tom and I looked at each other.

"Rings?" Tom said. "Do we need rings?"

"You didn't get rings?" she asked.

We had no answer. In the rush of everything we had to get done, rings weren't even on the list.

"Let's get in the car," his mother said wisely. "We'll find a shop that sells jewelry. Because yes, Tom, you absolutely need rings."

The next day was Tom's graduation. He marched in the cap and gown parade across campus, shook hands with the chancellor, and received his diploma. Afterward there was an outdoor buffet, and the world was all smiles.

As afternoon turned into evening, several of Tom's Comco friends converged on him. They all had brand-new shiny degrees, and Tom was about to get married. With so much to celebrate, they were determined to throw him a bachelor party—Alaska style.

"We've got a canoe," said Ron Brooks. "We're going boating."

I reminded Tom that my parents were due to arrive the next morning, the day of our wedding. Not only was their daughter getting married but, after years of enjoying Alaska from a distance through my letters and calls, they finally were going to see it for themselves. I didn't want anything to go wrong.

"Don't worry," said Tom. "I'll be back tonight, not too late."

As they went out the door, I asked, "Where is this boat?"

"On the Chena River," said Joe Head. "We're going to stop at every bar along the way."

In Fairbanks, that would require quite a few stops.

Tom didn't come home that night or the next morning. The wedding was hours away and I had no idea where he was—no message, no phone call, no sign of him anywhere. I drove to the airport, wondering how I was supposed to have a wedding without the groom.

As I collected my mom, dad, and my sister Christine, I saw a familiar shape at the airport terminal. It was Joe Head, passed out in a chair and reeking of stale beer.

"Joe," I said, grabbing his collar. "Where is Tom? Where is he?"

"He's by the river," said Joe, "in a cabin."

"What cabin? What's the address? What street?"

"It doesn't have a name," he said, and then passed out.

We carried Joe to my station wagon and laid him in the back next to the spare tire. At every intersection, someone would shake him awake. He would raise his head, look around groggily, and point left, right, or straight ahead. Then he would fall asleep again until the next intersection when someone would wake him again.

After forty minutes of this, at the time when I should have been getting into my wedding dress, we drove down a dirt road that turned into a narrow set of ruts along the river. At the end was a small cabin.

I went to the door and knocked.

I heard someone groan. This wasn't exactly an invitation to enter, but my patience was beyond gone. Inside, the cabin was a mess, with guys in their underwear passed out everywhere—on the floor, under the table, and one draped from a shelf that folded down from the wall.

I felt someone behind me, horrified to realize that my mother had followed me in. She stared at the log walls and plank floor of the cabin, lined with half-naked young men.

"This is so charming," she said. "It's right out of *Heidi*."

Then she turned to me. "Mary, dear, which one is yours?"

～◦

Two hours later, with Tom clean and sober, we drove up Ester Dome to the lodge. I had everything I was supposed to bring: the cake, the pair of gold rings from J.C. Penney, and the groom. Despite his late night, Tom looked cheerful and pleased in his handsome new suit.

As I got out of the car, I was flanked by my bridesmaids, our long skirts billowing in the wind making us look like a trio of bells; I really was the belle of this ball.

In her pink ruffled outfit, Tom's little sister Andrea ran over to join us, carrying her flower-girl bouquet. Then the best man, Karl Hanneman, approached wearing a sharp-looking green vest.

"I don't have a tie," he said. "What should I do?"

"I've got a spare," said my dad. He showed Karl how to put it on. Born and raised in Alaska, Karl had never worn a tie.

With everything in place, we made our entrance. Inside the log chalet, the first guest to greet me was a woman I had never seen.

"You don't know me," she said, "but I met your friend at the grocery store and she asked what I cooked best. Here it is—my grandmother's special potato salad. I only made a double batch. I hope it's enough."

I was so moved. To me, this was Alaska's real charm—that it was a place where a complete stranger could come to your wedding, bringing her very best. But in this land of extremes, the flip side was never far away. Tacked to the wall beside my new friend was a note the owner had posted for trespassers. The written words that greeted every one of my guests, said, "If you can read this, stay out or I'll shoot you dead. If you don't believe me, ask around."

We marched by his death threat to the strains of my wedding music playing on a squeaky cassette. The ceremony was simple and brief. After the vows were said, the preacher invited our guests to speak up and say why we *should* be married. Many of our friends said touching, impromptu things.

With the toasts all said, my piano music serenading the guests, and the table layered with food, I thought it was time for the party. Not quite.

"Stop the music!" Dr. Turner called out. With his six-foot-two frame and arms upraised, he almost touched the ceiling.

I was not pleased. I knew my boss occasionally enjoyed a bit of grandstanding. But I never expected he would highjack my wedding.

"Ladies and gentlemen," he called out. "I have an important announcement to make."

Good grief. What was he up to? Why hadn't he taken his turn making a toast like everyone else?

"As many of you know, Mary took her comprehensive exam on Friday," he said. "We didn't think we would get the results back so soon, but our visiting dignitary, Sir Edward Bullard, all the way from England and knighted by the Queen, helped with the grading. The test has now been thoroughly reviewed, and I'm pleased to announce that Mary has PASSED!"

What a wedding present! Sir Bullard, one of the world's most prominent geophysicists, deemed me worthy!

The distinguished gent with white ruffled hair raised the first toast. He and Lady Bullard were not the only dignitaries who came to our wedding. Tom had graduated with honors and at the awards dinner had invited the chancellor, Dr. Howard Cutler, and his wife Enid to our wedding. They came with smiles and a potluck dish like everyone else.

I looked around at all the shining faces, our families so happy, the professors so wise, and our newly degreed friends. Our futures stretched brightly in front of us. These people around me, this generation of adventurers, would explore the last corners of Alaska. The sky was the limit; there was nothing we couldn't do. Never again would people like us, ordinary people, be able to cast such long shadows over so vast a land.

We danced the night away, eager for all of our tomorrows, unaware that with great reward comes great risk.

I did not yet understand that our dreams came with a price.

18.

❧ Frontier Honeymoon ☙

$\mathcal{I}$ PLANNED TO REMAIN AT THE LODGE until the guests had gone home. We needed to clean up after the party and return the key to the owner. But our friends wouldn't stand for it.

"Go!" someone said. "Get out of here. We'll clean up."

"What about the key?" I asked. "We have to return it."

"I'll get it back," said a friend. "Don't worry about a thing. And don't go back to your apartment. You need a romantic getaway at a fancy hotel."

We had not planned to go anywhere special that night, but our apartment *was* full of house guests. So Tom and I headed for town looking for the best hotel we could find.

At the end of the oil pipeline boom, Fairbanks was still a Wild West town. The classiest hotel we could find had red velvet walls, ceiling mirrors, and cigarette burns on the bedspread. That night it also had thieves in the parking lot that broke into our trunk and took the only thing in it—the spare tire. The next morning, still in my wedding dress, I spent the first morning of married life climbing around a fifteen-foot mountain of rubber behind the car graveyard, looking for a tire that would fit.

Later, back at the apartment, we discovered that the key to the ski lodge had not been returned. The owner was upset and threatening to keep our deposit. We drove off to find the friend who had promised to return the key. We found him at his house, hung over and limping.

"What happened?" I asked. "Why didn't you return the key?"

"I couldn't," he said. "After you left, we all went up on the roof and I sprained my ankle."

"The roof?" I said. "What were you guys doing on the ski lodge roof?"

He shrugged. "Jumping off it."

Silly me for asking.

After we returned the key, it was time for the honeymoon. For this we took our families, nine of us in two cars, three hundred miles (480 km) down the Parks Highway to Anchorage. We drove through high mountain passes and spotted moose grazing in the foothills. As we swept through thick pine forests and wide valleys, we showed our families our special places—a frozen waterfall that Tom had climbed, the river by Carol's cabin, and the distant white crown of Sugar Loaf Mountain that I knew so well. Tom had a way of making the landscape come alive for our parents. For the first time they truly understood why we came and why we stayed.

~

After the guests went home, Tom flew off to the Seward Peninsula, a remote region of western Alaska separated from Siberia by the Bering Strait to work for the Anaconda exploration company. I stayed in town that summer to work on my data. I also needed to finish the geothermal map for Dr. Turner. It was growing so big that it spilled over the edge of the double-wide drafting table.

I moved into a shack I rented for cheap behind Yvonne's cabin. It was an old storage shed without even a woodstove. It was so rough that it made my bog cabin look like a plywood palace. But during those sunny days of summer, I didn't need more than a roof and four walls.

About this time, the university was experimenting with new technology—a computing machine designed to "process" text. In a special room, three computers were wired to a printer that stamped out the words with a rotating ball, one letter at a time. These machines were temperamental and became overloaded easily. They crashed often, losing every bit of their content.

I became one of the first geology students to try it and write my thesis on a computer. My first draft was not very good. My second wasn't much better. It seemed to me there was some coded language that I didn't understand for writing scientific text.

With further revisions, the thesis began to take shape, with proper citations, figures, and pages of graphs.

Meanwhile, Tom and another geologist, Mark Zdepsky, discovered a world-class deposit of tin in the Kougarak Mountains not far from

Nome. Leave it to Tom to make a major discovery. Whatever the job requires, he has always had a way of making things happen.

By the end of the summer, I had finished Dr. Turner's geothermal map and picked up two more jobs. During the day I worked for the U.S. Bureau of Mines sorting claim data; at night, I taught geology classes at Fort Wainwright, the nearby army base.

When Tom returned in the fall, we rented a cute log cabin near the campus with all the amenities. It even had a funky fish tank built into a log wall. It was the perfect place to start our married life, except for one thing: it wasn't ours. Could we afford to buy a house? Consulting our bank statements, we thought that if we found a good deal, maybe we could.

The hunt was on.

19.

✎ Kozy Cabin ✎

PORING THROUGH THE CLASSIFIEDS that winter of 1979-80, one for-sale advertisement stood out: "Kozy Cabin in the Hills." We liked the sound of that. The cabin was up on Chena Ridge, an easy drive to campus. In the Chena Hills, the winter temperatures could be ten degrees warmer than those in the lowlands; in a sub-zero climate, that difference was a big plus.

A few weeks before Christmas, we called to inquire about the "kozy" cabin. The real-estate agent told us we would have to wait until January because the house was not ready for viewing. We made an appointment for mid-January.

That winter was a cold one. After a particularly cold night, we went to see the house for the first time. It was -30 F (-34 C) when we arrived at two in the afternoon, the sun already low and the day masked in twilight.

Set back into a snowy stand of cottonwood trees, the cabin was a steep A-frame, a huge triangle with barely any walls at all. There was no garage, but the narrow front deck faced due south, with a view that rolled out before us all the way to the Alaska Range. We couldn't wait to see the inside.

When the agent pried the door open, we were shocked to be hit by a blast of air that was even colder than the outside. Tom whispered to me that if the house had retained the extreme cold of the previous night, the insulation must be good.

The power was off and it was dark inside. As our eyes adjusted in the dim light, we saw one big room with a soaring ceiling and a loft set into heavy brown cross-beams. But we couldn't see the floor. It was covered with broken furniture, shattered dishes, torn clothing, and shredded paper. Cementing the knee-high carpet of trash was a thick layer of *something*. It looked like frozen cake frosting, and was suspiciously brown.

It was animal waste, covering every inch of the floor.

The agent groaned and retreated to her car. In her sling-back heels, she wasn't equipped to negotiate the mountains of rubbish or deal with the cold, a blistering -40 F (-40C) temperature *inside* the house.

Tom and I climbed over the trash piles, careful not to slip on the brown "ice" as we waded through the remnants of what we later learned had been an ugly divorce.

Upstairs in the loft we found a different kind of trash. Here the debris was mostly broken liquor bottles, covering the floor with several inches of broken glass.

At the back of the house was a jagged hole that had been ripped through the back wall, exposing the solid construction around us. Here we could see for ourselves the sturdy timbers supporting the frame, exposing a section of pink insulation an impressive twelve inches thick. Tom, a third-generation engineer, was positively beaming.

We caught up with the embarrassed real-estate agent at her car. She was so upset she could barely speak. All we could coax from her was that the seller, Woody Jones, had promised the house would be warm and clean for the viewing.

Tom and I didn't need to confer; we were already on the same page, the only two people in all of Fairbanks crazy enough to make an offer for the place. Unlike some of our carpenter friends, we weren't able to build our own house, but we could clean this one. And given its state, the price had to come down. This was the bargain we had been looking for.

We met Woody Jones. He promised to clean out his junk and pay the penalty fee for letting the electricity bill expire. He never did. We bought the house anyway, prepared to deal with the mess. But in the cold night of winter, it didn't occur to us that when we fired up the woodstove and thawed the house out, we would have something much worse to contend with—the smell.

On the first day of cleanup, we awoke in our clean little rental house and lingered over our eggs and toast, putting off the arduous task that faced us on Chena Ridge.

As we pushed our eggs around on our plates, our spirits sagged.

Our friends told us we were out of our minds to buy that disaster. Where they right? What had we been thinking?

The doorbell rang and it was big Ron Brooks and his pickup truck loaded with shovels, rakes, and a pick-ax, all mining tools for chipping and hauling away mine waste debris. For this cleanup, nothing less would do.

"What are you waiting for?" said Ron. "Let's go."

Tom and I couldn't believe it. Someone was volunteering to help. Ron's spirit was just what we needed. We climbed into his truck and drove up Chena Ridge to our new house where Ron cheerfully joined us in the mucking-out process.

Growing up on a farm I had shoveled out barns full of horse and cow manure—not the most pleasant of tasks. But those animals are vegetarians, and their waste has the ripe but earthy smell of fermented greens.

The odor here was much worse because this waste came from dogs, carnivorous creatures, and their dung includes bowel-processed dead meat. If you've ever stepped in it, you know what I mean. Here we had layers of that soaked into dozens of square yards of rubbish, in all stages of decay.

With rags tied around our faces to filter out the rotting-waste odor, we hacked the garbage into chunks with the pick ax and hauled it away, truckload after truckload. After a while, the process felt like an archeological dig, each new layer revealing more clues about the people who had lived here and the circumstances that had led the house to this state. From the moldy receipts to the discarded bottles and clothes, we pieced together the sad story of a man named Woody Jones.

Apparently, Woody trained as a pilot and married Cora Jean, his sweetheart from Georgia. They moved to Fairbanks and bought the cabin to start their new life together. For a while, everything was rosy. He made good wages, and they got a puppy. But as Woody's job took him away for long spells, Cora Jean became lonely and bought another dog, and another, until they had six dogs and two cats.

When she was not collecting pets, Cora Jean lined her kitchen shelf with salt and pepper shakers shaped like toilets, some with attached buns. The pair also collected mugs with rude sayings, including one cup that was shaped like a breast that said "drink your milk."

Then Woody injured his back and no longer could sit in a cockpit for long flights. Forced to change careers, Woody moved to a specialty he apparently knew quite a bit about—alcohol.

Sadly, being a liquor distributor was not the dream job he expected. Frustrated by the reduction in pay, he took to drinking his inventory. He used the loft as a convenient place to chuck the bottles. Judging from the amount of shattered bottles we found, it appears he enjoyed the cathartic sound of breaking glass.

Life was now conspiring against Woody, and Cora Jean was not happy. The quarrels got louder and meaner. When words weren't enough, he had his gun. We don't know if she was in the house when he fired it, but we traced the path of his bullet holes through the loft's banister and out the ceiling.

Cora Jean went back to Georgia, leaving the pets behind. Unable to care for himself, much less the animals, Woody left the cats and the dogs locked in the house with a bucket of water and sacks of dry food to last them a while. But they did not last long enough.

When the food ran out, the dogs ripped the house apart. In desperation, they chewed their way outside, promptly killing and eating a neighbor's dog. Animal control officers were called in and the dogs, by then wild beyond redemption, were destroyed. As for the cats hidden in the loft, one froze to death and the other lost both ears to frostbite.

It was in this madhouse of abuse and neglect that Tom and I made our first real home together, determined not to follow in Woody Jones' path.

After several truckloads of garbage went to the dump, we could finally see the floor—an orange shag carpet splotched with stains. But even with everything cleared out, the smell remained as repulsive as ever.

Tom wanted to have the rug cleaned. I wanted to rip it out.

Tom pointed out that a carpet-cleaning allowance had been negotiated in the price of the house. If we didn't use it, we would lose it.

He was adamant, so I agreed to give it a try. The rug cleaner arrived in his white lab coat with a machine as big as a bathtub. With its thick hoses, it soaked and sucked every inch of the filthy shag. The rug turned a bright orange, and all we could smell was disinfectant.

The next day, the ammonia drifted away, and the smell of rotting dog waste returned. It hadn't been removed after all; it had only been masked. Still, Tom did not want to "waste" our meager funds on a new carpet.

"We'll clean it ourselves," he said. The "we" ended up being me going to the store and buying a shopping cart full of every rug-cleaning product available—foams, sprays, and powders. I applied them all, using so much powder that the orange carpet turned white. Then I vacuumed it all.

Clouds of toxic white dust rose from the rug. I ran out of the house choking, my eyes tearing. From outside I couldn't see in through the windows because the cloud of white vapor was so thick. It didn't dissipate for three days. When it finally cleared, I went in. But the rotting smell persisted as strong as ever.

"Try the powder again," said Tom, ever so helpfully.

No way. I was done with carpet cleaners. This sorry rug was too far gone.

Still Tom wouldn't concede. "A multi-million dollar industry like carpet cleaners can't be all wrong." he said.

I was in no mood to debate his "logic." I just wanted to breathe in my own house without feeling sick. But as long as that disgusting rug was still there, this wasn't going to happen.

Tom wouldn't budge, so there was only one option left. I headed to the car.

"Where are you going?" he asked.

"To the Army base," I told him. "They like me out there. They hired me to teach that geology course. I'm sure I can enlist. I'll get a bunk in the barracks that doesn't smell bad. You can visit me on the weekends."

I was not bluffing.

"Wait," he said. "I've got an idea. Let's get rid of the rug."

We ripped out the orange carpet and the foam pad supporting it. The floorboards beneath were coated in layers of mold in all shades of gray-green. We scrubbed the wood on our hands and knees with wire brushes and bottles of bleach. We didn't stop until those floorboards were scraped raw, the top layers removed and the rest bleached a dull white.

Then we laid down a new rug, a bright sapphire blue as cool as the ocean. But the best part of all was the smell—it had none at all.

We thought we were finished with Woody Jones. But, as we would find, his legacy lingered.

In the three weeks of repairs before we could move in, people noticed the smoke rising from the chimney and dropped by. Some were looking for Woody. Apparently Woody had been skilled at getting people to lend him money, but was not very good at paying it back. His creditors wanted to know where he was. We couldn't help them. We were glad he had dropped off our radar.

Then the neighbors came around, curious with questions. One woman sheepishly asked if we had discovered anything odd.

"You mean the bullet holes?" I said, showing her the little round holes in the railing, the walls, and the ceiling.

"I knew it!" she cried. "My husband didn't believe me when I said there were gunshots coming from *inside* the house."

Another neighbor warned us that just because we lived nearby, we shouldn't expect any special favors from her husband who had too many clients to take any more. I had never heard of her husband, and was too embarrassed to ask what he did. Later I found out why he was considered to be part of the Fairbanks elite—he was the best plumber in town.

A few days before we were scheduled to move in, Tom and I were having breakfast at our rental house when I got an unexpected phone call.

"What is it?" said Tom.

"I don't believe it," I told him. "A lady on the phone wants to come over and pick up Woody's things for him. She says she's a friend."

What nerve of this man to abuse his animals, trash his house, lie about fixing it, and then wait until after we had bought and cleaned his mess before sending someone over to randomly claim things. If this woman was a friend, where had she been when those dogs needed feeding? What kind of friend allows your cats to freeze to death?

"Hand me the phone," said Tom. "I'll take care of this."

I passed it over, glad to put his authoritative male voice on the line.

"Yes," he told the woman. "Today will be fine. Come over and take anything you like."

I couldn't believe it. This was the same Tom who had fought so hard to keep the hideous rug. Now he was inviting these people back into our house to take whatever they wanted.

"What are you thinking?" I asked.

"We need to be done with these people," he said. "Let them take whatever they want, and get them out of our lives for good."

He had a point. Maybe this woman needed to learn exactly what kind of friend Woody Jones really was.

I drove up to the house to meet her. She arrived with several cardboard boxes in tow. I thought she would be pleased to see how we had restored the place her friends had once called their home.

"What happened to the chair that went here?" she asked, sniffing her nose in dismay.

"It was trashed by the dogs," I told her. I didn't add that they had chewed out the stuffing, flipped it over, and then shit on what was left of the cushion.

She scowled. "What about the floor mat that went here?"

Floor mat? Woody Jones wouldn't have asked for a floor mat, and this friend certainly wasn't going to mail a used door mat to Cora Jean in Georgia. This woman wasn't here for the Joneses after all; she was here for herself, hoping to grab whatever she could. From what we knew about Woody Jones, I shouldn't have been surprised.

As she looked around, she complained that we hadn't saved more. How selfish of us, not to treat her friends' things with more respect.

I barely managed to keep a lid on my temper, a trait I inherited from the Scottish side of my family. My father and I both had a tendency to anger quickly. Many years later when he was dealing with cancer, the last thing he said to me was that we shared the same temper. I think it gave him some comfort to know that something about him would live on, even if it wasn't his favorite trait.

Woody's friend made her way to the kitchen cabinet where she found the collection of tasteless mugs and salt and pepper shakers. These things had survived because they had been on a high shelf out of reach of the dogs.

"I'll just help myself to these," she said, putting them into a box.

When she had cleaned off the shelf, she looked around for more. But there was nothing left. She glared at me.

"What a shame," she said with a heavy sigh, staring down at the jumble of ceramic toilets and rude body parts. "Here they are, in this box, all their hopes and dreams. All that remains of their loving union."

It took all my restraint not to laugh. Clearly, this woman and the tit mug were made for each other.

With the shelves cleaned out and nothing left for her to take, I escorted her to the door. She paused on the threshold and looked up.

"Do you have a ladder?" she asked.

"Why?" I asked, fairly sure I wouldn't like the answer.

"I'd like to climb up there and take that light fixture with me."

"We bought that light fixture," I said.

"Well," she huffed, "there was one there before. I don't know what you did with it."

From outside on our deck, she noticed our two dogs in their doghouse, surrounded by a fence that extended far back into the woods, giving our dogs plenty of room to run.

"Do you have some tools?" she said. "I'd like to take that fence with me."

"I built that fence," I told her. The only dog fence Woody Jones had provided for his pack of dogs was one small pen not much bigger than a closet.

"You didn't build the gate, did you?" she said.

I didn't reply. I was finished with her. She wasn't getting anything else from me—no light bulbs, no chicken wire, not another word.

I slammed the door, hearing her mutter, "I suppose it *would* be a lot of work to take it apart."

I watched her truck leave my driveway, taking with it her box of miniature toilet glory. Tom was right; it was better with that stuff gone.

Now our house was a blank canvas. We scoured the newspaper ads for used furniture, and prowled the home-improvement stores. We tiled our kitchen counter, removed the tin fireplace, and installed a furnace. We found a service to truck in water twice a month into a holding tank in the back. We even installed a stained-glass window above the front door, like the one in Carol's McKinley Park cabin, which split the sun beams into rainbows of color. We made that A-frame chalet so charming that I never wanted to live anywhere else.

We had purged the spirit of Woody. Except for the bullet holes piercing the walls, there was no more trace of him in our home.

A few years later I heard a radio announcement for a wet tee-shirt contest. The advertisement promised a free drink to all female contestants. In those early pipeline days, a lady didn't need a wet tee-shirt to get a free drink in a bar. It was such a bad idea on so many levels, especially in the winter, that I turned up the radio to hear more. What financial genius thought he could make money on this? Who was this misguided sultan of sleaze?

The promoter and judge was our own Woody Jones.

20.

⤜ In My Defense ⤚

$\mathcal{A}$S WINTER MELTED INTO SPRING, my old Datsun's engine finally gave out. To replace it, I bought a mud-ugly but solid Landcruiser Jeep, the same type that had surprised me out in the tundra north of Ferry. Those hunters had been right; this model was a sturdy off-roader. Tom would borrow my jeep for staking jobs and bring it back, the engine still running, with sapling trees sticking out of the hood.

During this time I continued to nibble away at my thesis until I had parts of every aspect written on paper. Arranging the pieces allowed me to build the framework that would present the thesis as a unified whole. Once all the chapters were finally complete, more than one hundred pages in all, it looked right. My advisers agreed. I had the stack of pages copied and bound and turned it in for review. Then, holding my breath, I scheduled my thesis defense—the last hurdle I would have to clear to earn my master's degree.

I have heard that more people are afraid of public speaking than dying. At some universities, you can avoid a public presentation of your work by arranging a small private session with your committee. At the University of Alaska, we didn't get to choose; we had to do both.

I would be speaking in the Brooks Building's big lecture hall. Anyone was welcome to come and ask questions. To pass, I would have to dazzle the audience, and convince them I was the world authority on those rocks. At the same time, I wasn't to speak down to them. Not all the people judging me would be geologists. One of the people chosen for the panel would be a professor from a different field. I risked failure if I talked over his head or confused him with jargon.

When the public presentation was over, the audience would leave and the big double doors would close behind them, locking me in with the panel of examiners. These were the men and women who would decide that day if I would earn my degree. I knew from watching other students who had gone before me, their faces pale as they came out of that room, that the margin for error was very thin.

If a student was too full of himself, the committee's job was to take him down a peg. At the same time, if a candidate hesitated, they would smell the weakness and tear him apart. I had seen both outcomes, and they were not a pretty sight.

I did what I could to prepare while counting down the days to that scary red circle on my calendar, the day of my thesis defense.

That morning finally arrived in May of 1980, exactly one year after our wedding, I woke early. Was I ready? Had I done enough? Should I go over everything one last time? I decided not to. If I wasn't ready by then, no last-minute cramming was going to save me. But I had to do something to calm down my nerves.

Unable to eat breakfast, I turned on the TV for inspiration. We had a small black and white set with a tinfoil antenna that received three stations, so I was not expecting much. I found a soap opera that was dreadfully cheesy—and exactly what I needed. Watching the bad acting with the forced dialogue took the edge off my jitters like a shot of Novocain straight to my nerves.

The lecture hall in the Brooks Building was full. Who were all these people? Was our tight little geo-world really this big?

As I entered the room with my slides and notebooks of research, the noise fell to a hush. I marched up to the podium and stared out at the sea of expectant faces. As my first slide went up on the screen, I wondered why I had worried about this part. After all, it was just teaching, and I was at home with that.

I went through my story about those three piles of rocks, each with its own history, not related at all. I answered the questions. It wasn't as hard as I thought it would be. I had been there and had spent the last two years thinking of little else. I spoke for my rocks and gave them a voice.

Then the room emptied and I was left with the small group that held the fate of my career in their hands. I discovered that I was not afraid. I knew my rocks. I had breathed in their dust, chipped at their outers, and pounded away at their core. I had sliced them open and peered into their tiniest crystals until I knew what they were and what they were not. I understood the forces that created and shaped them. And I had a suitcase of data beside me to back up everything I said.

Was I convincing? As the questioning went on, I could feel no holes in my knowledge that compromised my thesis defense. I had done my job; I had fortified the wall.

Finally, the panel sent me out of the room while it deliberated. I was told to come back in twenty minutes. I waited alone in the hallway, but sensed my friends peeking around the corner. They didn't want to jinx me.

Exactly twenty minutes later, I went back in to face the thesis committee, these respected experts all stern and serious. It's part of the ritual. I was told that I had passed, and we adjourned for the final step in the process—the celebratory round of beers at the campus pub.

As my friends gathered around, it slowly sank in what I had just done. It was just under three years since I had arrived in the state, and now I had a degree I had not expected, offering me entry into a career that topped my best dreams. In fact, compared to my real life, my nightly dream world seemed dull. Although I was still in my early twenties, I had found a life partner with a matching love of adventure, an understanding of work in the field, and a shared vision for the life we would build together in the north. I had a jeep that could get into tough places and a house near the crest of Chena Ridge with a hundred-mile view.

Could it get any better than this? Why not? After all, this was Alaska. Up here, anything was possible, right?

As the spring daylight grew longer, we prepared our house for summer guests. Making arrangements wasn't easy because our house didn't have a telephone. In those days before cell phones, Fairbanks had a shortage of phone lines. Even our neighbor, the state senator, couldn't get a phone line put in. So Tom got a pager. It would beep at any hour of the night and Tom would get up and drive 2.7 miles (4.3 km) to the bottom of the hill to a gas station where he would drop a quarter into a pay phone and call the pager company to retrieve his message. This system was better than nothing, but not by much.

Our first guest was my younger sister Stephanie. I was glad she could visit because she was thinking about becoming a geologist, too. I was able to get her a field assistant job that summer with the PhD student who had rented the bog house after me. The job didn't pay much, but Stephanie would get valuable experience to help her make a career decision.

Tom ran a small crew out of the historic Nabesna mining camp near the Canadian border about four hours' drive south of Fairbanks. There he analyzed the old tailing piles, looking for remnants of gold the early-century miners had missed with their primitive equipment. Tom hired his brother, Frank Albanese from New Jersey, who stayed at our house when he wasn't at the mine. Big Ron Brooks was also part of that crew along with a hitch-hiker the guys picked up out on the Alaska Highway. This hitch-hiker was a good worker when he wasn't trying to kill himself over the girl who had jilted him. One morning when the guys had come in from the mine, I found the hitch-hiker under my sink searching for a box of Drano to drink.

After hiding my industrial-strength cleaners, I put him to work on a carpentry job. In the high rafters near the peak of our house, he made a beautiful miniature loft, just big enough to sit in, like the crow's nest on a ship.

Ginger, our husky-collie dog, had a litter of eight puppies that summer, delivering them on the softest place she could find—Frank's duffel bag. For days Tom's poor brother had to clean afterbirth out of his tee-shirts and jeans.

I worked on two field jobs that summer for Jim Barker with the Bureau of Mines. First, I went northeast to Circle, named for its proximity to the Arctic Circle, to scout for salt-like deposits. I chartered a helicopter and flew over the flats looking for ponds with white rims of evaporated crusts. When I spotted one, we'd drop in and sample what was there. I was the crew chief for that job. Exploring for evaporated mineral deposits was satisfying work because the results were apparent so quickly. With evaporates, only three questions mattered—how wide, how deep, and how pure.

For the second job, I went northwest to the Selawik Hills, a low-lying range north of Nome. The Selawik crew consisted of me and three men. I bunked in a pup tent with Steve Will, who had been married to my friend Laurel from the boot camp for geology students in the Brooks Range two years before.

The tent provided by the Bureau of Mines was dismally small. Even if we left our packs outside, there wasn't enough room for both of us to sleep flat on our backs. We had to lie on our sides.

I had the perfect room divider—my good old shotgun Sally. I put it lengthwise between us to define our separate spaces. Still, with so little room, sleeping was difficult. Tundra looks fuzzy, but it's not. It is prickly and uneven and as comfortable as lying on basketballs made out of wicker.

Early one morning, about an hour before we were supposed to get up, I woke with a terrible muscle cramp. To work it out, I *had* to lie flat on my back, but I needed more room. I was desperate.

I slid the shotgun over an inch into Steve's side, wedging it under his sleeping bag.

"Steve," I said. "Wake up. What are you doing? You're on my side."

"Sorry," he mumbled, and moved closer to his wall of the tent.

This worked so well that I tried it again.

"Steve," I said. "You're on my side again."

"Okay," he muttered, inching over a little more.

I couldn't believe it worked twice in a row. It was too easy. I couldn't resist.

"Steve!"

With Sally's iron barrel beneath him, he scooted over once more. By now, he was jammed up against the edge of the tent, his entire body flat against the tent fabric. From the outside of the tent, Steve would have looked like a statue with his profile perfectly etched in green nylon.

I got one blissful hour of sleep fully flat on my back. It was just what I needed.

A few days later, my shotgun sprang apart as I hiked along a rocky arctic marsh. The threads holding the barrel to the stock had given out and the coiled spring released, sending pieces of Old Sally flying across the tundra. I got down on my hands and knees in the damp moss and found all the pieces. I tried to reassemble the shotgun but it was no use.

The threads of the barrel were stripped—I had literally worn out that gun. Poor old Sally had been scraped through too many miles of brush and drenched by too many rainstorms. All the gun oil in the world couldn't save her.

It was time to retire old Sally, my sawed-off friend that had spent so many days as my constant companion and ready defender.

Tom surprised me with an early birthday gift, a new snub-nosed .44 magnum pistol. I couldn't have asked for a better present. If any handgun could stop a charging bear, it was this Dirty Harry model. With the barrel trimmed down short just for me, my "Dirty Mary" fit into a hip holster tucked under my vest. Now, when I charged through the brush, there was no shotgun banging against my left shoulder to get caught on the branches.

I thought it would feel odd without that constant weight of a shotgun pulling on my left side, but in no time at all, I found I didn't miss it at all.

I doubt my tent-mate missed it, either.

21.

⚬ Mister Lucky ⚬

AFTER WORKING AT THE NABESNA MINE, Tom got a job with a local mining company, Resources Associates of Alaska. The company was started about ten years before when a few guys got together in their basements to sieve buckets of dirt looking for gold. This home-grown operation grew and merged into Northern Energy Resources Co. (Nerco), one of the biggest companies in Fairbanks. Tom's career grew with it.

Meanwhile, I was aiming for a career in the public sector. Although I enjoyed working for the Bureau of Mines, it wasn't my dream job. It wasn't where the bulk of the state's mapping was happening. That was over at the state Division of Geological and Geophysical Survey, or the Alaska State Survey for short.

It wasn't just the geologists working there who impressed me. The entire staff seemed to be on a mission to best serve the people of Alaska. Because of this, the Alaska State Survey attracted the most dedicated and talented people, not only geologists, but also the top chemists, lab technicians, and professional staff. Nearly everyone there had made extraordinary contributions to the state. Some of them had already left a legacy that extended beyond the geological world. One example of this was Anne-Lillian Schell, the chief cartographer. She had designed patterns, inspired by local artifacts, which were used in Alaska's qiviut trade, the warm and lacy soft musk ox wool products knitted by the native women in the villages.

In the fall of 1981, I heard the Alaska survey was hiring new geologists and I wasted no time applying. The first position went to someone else. So did the second one. But when a third position opened up, the state hired me. Now I was part of the Alaska State Survey, where so many giants of Alaska geology had forged their careers. From then on, I would work side by side with Holister Grant, Tom Bundtzen, and John Dillon. I already knew most of these proven explorers, and couldn't wait to see who they'd put me with first.

I was assigned to Jeff Kline, the only geologist at the Alaska survey that I hadn't met. I didn't even know what he looked like. The only thing I had ever seen of him was the cliff Holister Grant had showed me from the helicopter where Jeff had broken his back. I would be moving into his office, intruding on a space he was accustomed to having all to himself.

I went to introduce myself, nervous about my first day on the job, wondering what my new office would be like. When he opened the door, a wave of cigarette smoke slammed me, tinged with the smell of burned coffee. The room was worse than I could have imagined. His desk was so full of clutter that the top layers of aerial photos, maps, and pencils in every color balanced precariously like a stack of dominos about to topple over. On the side, a bookshelf was jammed indiscriminately with journals about to fall out. Behind the door was a small table with papers scattered around a glass coffee pot furiously boiling a strangely black sludge.

Jeff himself was too thin, his skin as pale as eggshells, with hair that flopped into his eyes instead of covering his ears.

"Sorry about the mess," he said as he stacked the stained papers around the coffee pot. "I'll have it cleaned up in a jiff."

Was he kidding? Cleaning up this debris would require more than just stirring it around.

Then I realized he was enlarging the coffee blast zone for a reason—this was where I was supposed to make my maps. My sanctuary for contemplative thoughts, for expanding the knowledge of the state's resource knowledge base, was a coffee stand.

When Jeff had cleared a few inches of bare table, the laminate surface marred with burns, he stood back with a proud smile.

"See?"

Yes, I saw.

I saw that I would be sweeping coffee grinds from the pages of my work.

I saw that my lungs, already rebelling, were not appreciating his smoke.

I saw that there was no room for a chair that would not be hit every time the door opened.

And I saw Jeff's smile light up his face like a flashlight.

There was something distinctly Yvonne-like about his apologetic greeting and his futile attempt to clean up his mess—and the absurd assumption that somehow, he had.

I looked at the table, then at Jeff. In that face, there was no room for a gram of artifice as he beamed, radiantly pleased with himself.

Yeah, I could do this. The table was just topography.

I could do this just fine.

22.

‑❧ The Fossil Doctors ❧‑

$\mathcal{O}$NE PROFESSOR WHO DID NOT COME to our wedding was Dr. Dick Allison, the Geology Department's paleontologist. Dr. Dick, as we called him, was a crotchety soul. The only time he seemed happy, although he didn't actually smile even then, was when he took part in the annual academic parade held with commencement when he marched across campus in his doctoral robes. On those occasions, the pride on his face was unforgettable.

Apart from that annual ceremony, he had no interest in social interaction. This was just as well. His social skills were nothing to brag about.

Although I spent a semester in one of his classes, I had never had actually talked with Dr. Dick until a week after my wedding when he stopped me in the hall. He had never singled me out for a conversation before, so I was surprised. I assumed he wanted to congratulate me for having just gotten married.

I assumed wrong.

"Mary," he said, "I wanted to tell you that I personally graded the stratigraphy section of your comprehensive exam, and I must say I didn't like your answers at all."

Stratigraphy is the study of layered formations, the type of rocks that hold fossils. At most universities, when you study this field, you learn about fossils and the classic formations that the rock epochs were named after, like the Devonian sections off the Devon coast, or the classic Jurassic layers from the Jura Mountains.

In Dr. Dick's course, however, stratigraphy was more than evolution and dating of rocks and the practical aspects of studying fossils. In his class it became a ponderous philosophical discussion. He would speak with great reverence about the inner meaning of fossil units. To me, it was like studying to be a surgeon by discussing the meaning of life. I once met a geologist who thought this approach was brilliant, but most of us never got it. I certainly didn't. His weighty pontificating just blew over my head.

I wasn't surprised to learn that he didn't like my response to "the deeper meaning of fossilized assemblages." I wasn't all that crazy about my answer, either—or the question.

"If it had been up to me," he continued, "you would have failed the whole comprehensive exam. I lobbied to fail you, but I was overruled."

"Oh," I said, unable to come up with any other response.

"I just thought I'd tell you," he said. "Just so you know."

"Got it," I said. "Now I know."

Without another word, he shuffled away, almost a waddle, with his nose tipped up into the air.

I guess I was supposed to have felt offended, and I tried to be, just a little, for his sake. But I couldn't take him seriously. Mostly I felt sorry for the man, to have to live with himself, and to filter his world through that attitude every day of his life.

The only other professor as grumpy as Dr. Dick was Dr. Carol Allison. She was also his wife. As curator for the university museum's fossil collection, she was the other important paleontologist on campus.

In those days it was a challenge to study paleontology at the university. You needed the expertise of the two reigning specialists on your committee, but it was impossible to take them both on because they fought like a pair of tigers, neither giving an inch. These two squabbled about everything down to the most trivial detail, and it seemed so strange to me that after a full day of their legendary quarrels, they went home to the same house.

Before Jeff joined the Alaska Geological Survey, one of his first jobs as a young geologist was working for Dr. Carol Allison at the University of Alaska Museum, where much of the wealth of Alaska's history was kept. The museum had been started by Otto Geist, an archaeologist and explorer who in 1926 was charged by the university president Charles Bunnell to build a series of collections worthy of a museum. Geist took his work to heart. By the time of his death in 1963, his collections were legendary. In addition to the materials displayed in the museum, numerous boxes of loose fossils were stored in the bowels of the campus basements. But for some reason, Dr. Allison didn't like the way Geist had collected his fossils. Geist had noted where the fossils were found but did not include detailed explanations of the particular layers of the stratigraphic units that held them. In all fairness, many of the units had not yet been labelled in the 1920s. Even so, Carol was incensed that the fossils were not "properly" identified. She decided that Otto Geist's fossils, which formed the backbone of the museum's fossil collection, were simply not up to her standards. So she assigned her young assistant, Jeff Kline, to rectify the situation. Her solution? She ordered Jeff to take those fossils, box after box of priceless artifacts of Alaska's prehistoric record, and grind them to dust.

Jeff was appalled. He tried to protest, but she wouldn't listen. She was the boss, and he had to comply. She could be outrageously intimidating if she didn't get her way.

One geologist, the volcanologist Dr. Juergen Kienle who was so helpful on my thesis committee, found this out the hard way.

Apparently Dr. Allison heard that Dr. Kienle had unearthed some interesting fossils not far from one of his volcanic craters. These fossils were ammonites, the spiralled shells that look like segmented snails. They had not been recorded previously in that part of the state, so she asked Dr. Kienle to retrieve some samples for her. In the spirit of good science, he agreed.

The next time he returned from the site, he presented her with several large and well-preserved ammonites for the museum, and she was quite pleased. Unfortunately, as they were chatting, he mentioned that he had kept a few for his own personal collection.

She went ballistic, insisting that he had no right to keep any for himself. As the curator of the University's fossil collection, she felt that gave her authority over *every fossil in the state*. She insisted that he was not allowed to keep anything and must give them all to her at once.

He ignored her demand. He had just done her a huge favor and it was his discovery. Did it really matter if a few fossils sat on his mantelpiece instead of leaving them stuck in the ground? So he walked away and left her there stewing. After all, what could she possibly do about it?

That night as he was getting ready for bed, he found out exactly how far she was prepared to go when the Alaska State Troopers came to his house with handcuffs.

"Open up, Dr. Kienle," they shouted as they banged on his door. "We have reason to believe that you have stolen government property, and we are instructed not to leave here without it."

He explained the situation, and they said they understood. But they told him they were afraid of what Dr. Allison would do if they returned without the fossils. They begged him to give them up so they wouldn't have to deal with her wrath.

Dr. Kienle surrendered the fossils, and her ego remained intact. But after that, few geologists would share their finds with her, and the wealth of the state's fossil discoveries went largely unreported.

Jeff never forgot about all those boxed trays full of fossils, millions of years in the making. As he thought about those irreplaceable windows to Alaska's past that were ground to dust, he dreamed of ways to show his outrage. He wished he could find a belt with an ammonite on the buckle that he could wear all over town—she wouldn't dare to take that! One year for his birthday, I glued a perfect ammonite onto a silver belt buckle plate. Jeff was thrilled with his gift and wore that belt buckle every day, his proud act of rebellion for all those fossils he had been forced to destroy.

~⁓⁓~

As prickly as she could be, Dr. Allison did one thing that I will always appreciate. In the spring when the snow started to melt, she took it upon herself to host a ladies-only tea party at her house. She invited teachers, staff, and students in the geoscience fields. In those days, there were just a handful of female geologists. In a field dominated by men, it was nice for a change one night a year to be surrounded by female colleagues who understood what it took to break in.

Some companies had a blanket policy not to hire women. They would tell you to your face that women were trouble and kindly invite you to apply elsewhere. At one job interview, the employer said he couldn't possibly hire me because he couldn't have me seducing his men. In those days, they got away with it. Even at the state survey, a government agency, women were hired at a much lower pay grade than their male counterparts.

When I joined the state survey, I was hired five pay-grades below a male colleague who, like me, had just received his master's degree.

He was given a spacious office and his own project to run. When I was hired two months later, I was assigned to be his Xerox girl. My job was to spend hour after hour, day after day, copying volumes of reference works from the library to fill up his book shelves. I was told this was the best use of my time because it saved him from having to buy his own reference books.

This went on for a few weeks until my vision became spotty from the constant flash of the photocopier light. My copying suffered, and there were sheets where the page numbers were cut off. The colleague complained to our section chief.

The section chief, another Dr. Dick, (I am not making this up) called me into his office and chewed me out for ten minutes. How dare I cut off the page numbers! Where was my *professional* pride? Didn't I realize these books were for someone important, a *man* with a *master's degree*? All the while, this Dr. Dick knew that I had earned the same degree since he had been consulted on my carbon dating.

Then his eyes flared like a cartoon villain as he snarled that I was in serious trouble because he was going to tell the big boss exactly what a bad copy girl I was.

Within minutes, the big boss called me into his office and asked me to shut the door. I felt sick. The big boss was Holister Grant who had championed my work in his journal. He was a man I respected, a man who had given me a job working here at the state survey. How, in one month, had I managed to screw it up?

Instead of firing me, Holister apologized. He said he had no idea what Dr. Dick was up to, wasting my talents as a human copier, and he promptly assigned me to other duties. For the rest of the winter, I worked in the microscope room, identifying the mineral components of rocks. This was so much better. Most of the project heads had more rocks than they had time to properly analyze themselves. With me assigned to the microscope room instead of to a specific person or a project, I could ask anyone on the staff if they wanted my help with their samples. This let me side-step the Dr. Dicks of the geology world and provide detailed thin section reports for the good guys.

I learned to navigate around the Dr. Dicks, but they never went away. I always felt their eyes on me, just waiting for me to make a mistake. With this daily work setting, it was satisfying to swap stories once a year with other women as we sat around Carol Allison's kitchen table sipping herbal concoctions. We didn't always talk about the burdens of gender. Sometimes it was good enough just to see all the women who had made it. Quite often, it was enough just to enjoy the tea.

23.

Jeff's Hush-Hush News

ONE ICY MONDAY MORNING, I told Jeff Kline about a dinner over the weekend where someone performed our favorite party trick—tossing a skillet full of hot water into the freezing air.

Jeff was amazed. He had never heard about this and couldn't wait to try it. He didn't have hot water but had plenty of coffee. He poured an inch of steaming coffee into a mug and we went up to the roof of the Geophysical Institute to see what would happen.

"Are you sure about this?" he asked.

"Just throw it up," I told him. "We did this all weekend, and nothing came down."

So he tossed the coffee high into the air. It came back down, every drop of it, all over his shirt. The mug broke at the handle, and the ceramic cup hit him, too.

Jeff looked so pitiful holding the broken handle of his favorite mug with coffee dripping down his clothes, that I was reminded why we called him Mister Lucky.

Not long after that, on another Monday morning, Jeff burst into the office, breathless from more than the cold. Something was up.

"I've got a secret," he said. "I bought something big, really big. But I'm not telling you what it is."

"You can't do that," I said. "You can't announce you have a secret that you're not going to tell."

"I *have* told somebody," he said. "I told Tom Bundtzen. And I'm going to tell Frank Larson. But I'm not telling you. It's a guy thing. You wouldn't understand."

These guys were all my friends, too. But Jeff was more like a brother, effortlessly shifting from a prince to a brat. Apparently, this was one of the bratty times.

Jeff never did tell me his secret. I had to hear fifth-hand that he had bought Kristin, one of our geological assistants, a diamond engagement ring. He had asked her *the* question and Kristin said yes!

There was just one problem. Kristin's parents disapproved of Jeff, even though he had a good job and worked hard. They didn't like the fact that he was divorced. They believed that without a proper Catholic annulment, his marriage to Kristin would amount to bigamy. As far as they were concerned, he might as well have had a dozen wives.

Jeff contacted the church and applied for an annulment. He booked counseling sessions with a priest, Father Jim, and then tracked down his ex-wife, who had moved out of the state. When he finally got her on the phone, he learned that she already had had their marriage annulled. Jeff was upset that she hadn't bothered to tell him, but at least he could get on with the wedding plans.

Still, Kristin's parents did not like Jeff. They flew up to Fairbanks the week of the wedding, but not as your typical guests. They came to stop it.

My job was to run interference on the day of the wedding. I was to make polite small talk with the parents and try to keep them out of the way. I arrived early at the church and found Jeff's face a shade whiter than usual.

"Kristin's brother is here," he said. "He went downtown and found a gun at a pawn shop. He plans to shoot me at the altar."

This put a kink in the schedule. Jeff and Kristin decided to sneak away with the priest and get married in a secret location. Meanwhile, I was supposed to stall the parents and gun-toting brother at the church.

I stood at the church's big double doors with one other usher, Kathy Goff, the former field-camp cook. She had finished her own degree and was working on a contract job for the state survey.

When the guests arrived, Kathy and I explained that the church wedding was off and sent them home. But Kristin's family never showed up. We worried that something had gone very wrong until Jeff called the church with good news. Father Jim had negotiated a solution. He explained to the parents that Kristin was going to go marry Jeff one way or another, and wasn't it preferable for the marriage to be sanctified in the church? Kristin's family agreed.

The church wedding was back on.

Kathy and I telephoned everyone we had turned away. By then it was late in the evening. Most of the guests returned, but not as elegantly dressed. One woman arrived in her pajamas.

The last to arrive was Kristin's family. We greeted them with our best smiles, all the while looking for suspicious bulges. We didn't see any. That was a good sign.

The ceremony was one of the briefest I've ever seen. Father Jim was taking no chances; in the service, he did not invite objections.

Afterward, everyone headed off to the reception. Kristin's family arrived later. The room went quiet as they handed Jeff a box from a Fairbanks pawn shop that we all knew sold only two things—guns and gold, a typical frontier combination. Expecting the worst, we crowded around as Jeff opened the box.

Inside was a solid gold coin. They hadn't purchased a gun, and Jeff's "shotgun" wedding became a solid gold wedding after all.

⁓

The next summer, I worked on a crew down in Hatcher Pass, a wide U-shaped valley north of Anchorage that had been gouged by ancient glacial sheets. This four-person crew consisted of me, Jeff and his bride, and the second Dr. Dick, my old Alaska Geological Survey section chief.

It was hard to get Jeff and Kristin out of their tent, young love and all, so I ended up working with Dr. Dick. He wasn't my favorite mapping partner. These weren't his kind of rocks, so he struggled to understand them. I taught him how to piece together the history of metamorphic rocks, and wasn't entirely surprised when he tried to take credit for "discovering" what I had showed him. What did surprise me was his daily lunch menu—a single raw turnip that he pulled out of a paper bag and ate raw like an apple.

Despite his low-maintenance food habits, he wasn't an easy camper. He refused to live out of a tent, and brought a motor home with him. This meant that we had to pitch our tents in a public campground by the road, complete with a water hook-up for Dr. Dick's camper. For safety reasons, because of the camp's public access, the helicopter couldn't be stationed there with us. It had to fly in from Anchorage every morning and then go back to the hangar at the end of the day.

It was the summer of 1981, barely a year after Mount Saint Helens erupted in Washington state. A shortage of helicopters existed that summer because so many aircraft had been sent to western Washington for the crews monitoring the eruption and its aftermath. We felt smug that we had chartered this helicopter from an Anchorage company and were securely locked into a contract.

On the ninth day of the project, we awoke as usual, ate a quick meal, and waited at the landing zone for our helicopter. It didn't arrive.

When it was three hours overdue, we piled into the truck and drove off to find a pay phone and call the charter company. We learned that some oil geologists had asked for a chopper and offered to pay extra. To accommodate them, the charter service sent them the only chopper in the hangar—*ours*. The charter company said that if we were lucky, we could have our helicopter the next day—unless, of course, the oil geologists needed it again. They'd let us know.

We were livid. How dare they take our money and resell our chopper time to someone else!

We railed at the wind. We shook our hands at the sky. We complained all day and all night until the next morning when once again, we waited in our field gear for our chopper to show up. It didn't.

As we kicked stones in frustration, Jeff turned on a radio and couldn't believe what he heard: A helicopter had crashed the previous day not far from our camp. We drove to a pay phone and called around. It didn't take long to find out that the downed helicopter was the one we had chartered. Apparently, it had flown through the ash cloud during the Mount Saint Helens eruption, a detail the charter service should have disclosed since ash is notoriously corrosive to engines. Soon after taking off the previous day, the engine had quit in the air and the aircraft crashed in a swamp with a full load of oil geologists on board. It was a miracle that no one was killed.

We should have been aboard. If we had been, flying over our mountains, we probably would not have been as lucky.

When the news spread, other field crews cancelled their contracts with this Charter service. Suddenly there was no shortage at all, and the company told us the "good news" that they found another helicopter for us that would pick us up the next day.

We weren't sure how to deal with all this. We jammed back into the truck and drove into town for a meal. We needed to talk.

Over a Chinese buffet, Dr. Dick argued that we should accept the second helicopter. We had to finish our work. We were already here in the field and the chopper time was paid for.

Jeff disagreed. Sure, we'd lose a few days of data and wouldn't get everything done. But this company had lied to us and treated us shamefully. Their choppers had *all* flown through the ash cloud and couldn't be trusted. He insisted it wasn't worth the risk.

Kristin Kline refused to vote. She did not want to choose between her husband and her boss.

The last vote, the swing vote, was mine.

The waitress came over to clear away our plates and leave the desert. We stopped talking and a long, awkward silence settled over us. This was no ordinary gathering for dinner. It was a guilty celebration that we hadn't died, and a life-or death decision that had dropped into my lap.

When the waitress headed back to the kitchen, all eyes turned to me.

"Well?" said Dr. Dick.

"Well?" said Jeff.

Kristin said nothing.

I didn't want to crash in the mountains. But I didn't want to leave a job unfinished either.

Jeff knew his mind and so did Dr. Dick. I wasn't sure, and it seemed strange that it was now my job to make this decision for everyone there. Whatever happened would be on my head.

So I did the only sensible thing: I reached for a fortune cookie, pulled out the little white strip of paper, and read these words:

Yesterday was dark, but tomorrow is bright once more.

"Get on your climbing boots," I said. "We are going to finish this job."

24.

⤜ Enter the Legend ⤛

WE COMPLETED OUR WORK AT HATCHER PASS early with no more helicopter problems and returned to Fairbanks with a month of summer left. I wasn't finished with field work for that season. Back in town, big news awaited.

Our office had hired a living legend—Dr. Thomas Smith, formerly the university's leading economic geologist. Dr. Smith was so respected in the mining industry that all the top mining companies vied for his thoughts on their rocks.

Nicknamed the Master of Confrontation, Dr. Smith was someone you didn't want to cross, the same formidable geologist who had mapped the Clearwater Mountains all by himself. At least that's how the story went.

I had my own history with Dr. Smith.

Years before, on my first field trip to the Brooks Range, Dr. Smith had walked up to me as I looked out over the arctic vista. Off in the distance was the trans-Alaska pipeline, a staggering feat of technology that would assure Alaska's economic health for decades to come. Back then, I wasn't impressed. I had not yet spent months living without heat and power and, like a lot of people, I took such comforts for granted.

Dr. Smith had asked me, "Isn't the pipeline an amazing achievement?" My reply was, "I think it's ugly, and they should get rid of it."

This, of course, did not endear me to the state's leading economic geologist. I have to admit there are times that I have a touch of Yvonne's "psychic disability," the uncanny talent to say exactly the wrong thing to the wrong person at the wrong time.

After making that comment, I never got a job with any of the mining companies that Dr. Smith had ties with, which seemed like just about every one operating in the state. I was thankful that our paths hadn't crossed in my career as a government geologist.

With him joining the Alaska Geological Survey, this was about to change.

⌒⌒

On his first day, Dr. Smith paced back and forth before us, a veteran general inspecting his troops.

"We're going to be mapping right here in town—the entire Fairbanks District," he announced. "There are pieces of old maps, but the whole district has never been done properly. I'll rotate around and work with each one of you. That way, I can see how you work and make sure you're all up to speed on how it should be done."

Great, a test.

There were at least twenty-five geologists and assistants in the room, the most I had ever seen working on a single mapping project. With safety in numbers, I figured I could still avoid Dr. Smith for a while. If I stayed low for a day or so, maybe I could get myself assigned to another project out of town for the rest of the summer. I hunched down behind someone. As the middle child, I was well versed in the art of being inconspicuous.

His eagle-eyes scanned the room. "And the person I'm going to work with first is … Mary! Tomorrow morning, 8 a.m. *sharp*, you're with me."

With a satisfied nod, he dismissed us and left.

The others picked up their things to go. I could sense their relief not to be the first one picked. They would be spared that distinction. They could go home that night secure in their jobs for at least one more day.

That night, I indulged in another one of my talents, and fretted entire kingdoms of worry.

⌒⌒

The next day proved to be every bit as awful as I had anticipated. It was almost noon by the time Dr. Smith and I got to the third outcrop.

Of course I knew how to work my compass. But why did it keep slipping from my hands?

"You're not supposed to measure the ground," said Dr. Smith. "You're supposed to measure the rocks."

It didn't seem possible, but the day kept getting worse. I was so nervous I could hardly function.

"And what's all that on your field vest?" he asked. "Your equipment is supposed to go inside your pack, not tied onto your vest."

Now he was convinced I didn't even look like a proper geologist with my field vest kitted out like a walking department store, my pockets bulging.

Then he looked at my field map. "And why is your writing so shaky?"

He was right; I could barely read it myself. Wasn't all that worrying supposed to prevent the worst thing from happening?

Disgusted, he wandered off and left me alone for the rest of the day, blissfully alone.

Back at the office that evening, he asked to see our field notes. We all put our yellow plastic notebooks in a pile on the table. Ignoring the rest, Smith plucked mine from the stack.

As he scanned the pages, his scowl lines grew deeper.

Then he spoke. "Mary, it says here that you found chert nodules."

"Yes," I managed to say.

"But the old map says you were in metamorphic terrain."

I nodded.

"Then you couldn't possibly have found a chert nodule, could you? Do you even know what a chert nodule looks like?"

"It looks like this," I said, removing a little round nugget from a sample bag tucked into my vest, a rock that on this first day of the project proved that the old map was wrong.

He stared at the rock and said nothing.

He didn't have to. I heard it without the words.

Maybe that blockheaded girl isn't such a blockhead after all.

25.

~ *Livengood* ~

*D*R. SMITH WAS A TOUGH BOSS, but he was fair-minded. He pushed us hard, but no harder than he pushed himself. He used to say that he didn't demand genius in his crew. He could do without that. What he couldn't stand was laziness, and he often said that he would take hard work over brilliance any day.

That summarized my geology career. I wasn't stellar, but I could work like a dog. He liked my work ethic. Despite our rocky start, we got along after all.

When I first joined the state survey, stationed at that table in Jeff's office, I had come down with asthma. At night, Tom could tell when I had spent the day in Jeff's office by how much I coughed. When I moved out of Jeff's office and into the microscope lab, my asthma went away.

I liked that I was no longer assigned to a particular section and could pick the crews I worked for, sometimes for Bundtzen, sometimes with Jeff. But after a while, I mostly worked for Dr. Smith, and that was fine with me.

In the summer of 1982, we ran a project out of Livengood, an hour north of Fairbanks on the Elliott Highway. At the time, this was the biggest field crew ever run by the Alaska Geological Survey with more than thirty people and Dr. Smith at the helm. Along with the geologists and assistants, we had a cook, a pilot, and a full-time mechanic to service the chopper. Each of us had our own tent—plastic domes held up by heavy steel rods, tall enough to stand up in, each with a portable kerosene heater. In the spacious work tent, we had folding chairs—with backs! Behind the camp, we had *two* outhouses, one for the gents and one for the ladies, even though there were only three of us.

Setting up a tent city in the wilderness is a massive job. A dirt trail led into camp from the gravel highway, but most of our supplies were brought in by helicopter. The equipment, lumber for the shelves, and personal items all were loaded into nets and air-lifted to the site, each sling-load dangling precariously below the helicopter.

After three days of setting up, our domed tents looked like a field of mushrooms. We had created an instant town in the middle of nowhere.

Then the mapping began. As ever, the field work was hard and, with Dr. Smith in charge, the days were particularly long. A typical day went like this:

I would wake up around six and throw on the same clothes I had worn the day before. Then I would amble into the big cook tent for breakfast. The cook tent was the cleanest place in the camp. No mud or rock samples were allowed. We scraped the dirt off our boots before entering. This was the only tent to have a "floor," a wide canvas tarp.

"Liz the Cook," we called her, taught French in the winter and could make just about anything on her kerosene stove, including freshly baked bread. She even cultured yogurt just for me, fresh every morning, because she knew I liked it. It boggled my mind that she could make bread and yogurt in a kerosene tent kitchen in the middle of the tundra.

After breakfast, around 6:30, people packed lunches for the day. But I didn't break for lunch. I couldn't afford to waste the time. Because my pace has never been fast, I worked through lunch so that I would cover as much ground as everyone else.

Skipping lunch wasn't my only trick. The backpacks we carried weighed about forty pounds at the start of the day, *without* rock samples. Mine was about ten pounds lighter because I pared down my survival gear to the bare minimum. Sometimes I wore my rubber rain gear, both the jacket and pants, even if it wasn't raining. It was easier to wear than to carry in the pack.

I never carried a full water bottle, either. Two inches of water was usually enough. As a hiker, I wasn't like a mountain goat that could sprint up a hill, but I did make a very good pack "camel."

After breakfast, we would gather in the work tent to plot our traverse for the day. This left a record of where we were supposed to be in case of emergency.

With our routes plotted, we took our packs to the helicopter to fly out in shifts, three or four at a time. We showed Chopper Mike where we wanted to be dropped off and marked the spot on his map where we expected to be at the end of the day.

If you were lucky, you would be dropped off in exactly the right spot. But sometimes there would be trees in the way, or the ground at the drop-off point was steeper than it appeared on the map. Then the pilot would drop you as close as possible, and you would have to start your day with an extra hike. We were glad that summer that we had Chopper Mike. He was an exceptional pilot, able to hold a hover on the side of a mountain, with the wind blowing, and get us in and out of tight places.

Once on the ground, the first thing to do was to call Chopper Mike on your radio to make sure you had two-way communication. Those big, heavy line-of-sight walkie-talkies were our lifelines.

On a typical day, you might cover about seven miles (11 km) of ground. Sometimes it was brushy, sometimes savagely steep. At every outcrop, we were to identify the rocks, measure angles, take samples, and mark everything on our maps. We took copious field notes, describing every aspect of the rock. We couldn't leave any observations out because we would never be back.

With rock hammers, we cracked open rocks all day long and peered into their inner layers. Our packs grew heavier as we collected more samples.

Even if metals weren't visible in the rocks, you might find traces of a deposit in the soil that washed into the creeks. To narrow in on possible finds, we collected stream-sediment samples, a fancy name for mud, at quarter-mile intervals along every streambed in the region. These bags of wet mud were as heavy as the rocks. It was not unheard of at the end of the day for a pack to weigh close to a hundred pounds. No wonder the doctors in town could always identify a geologist. We were the ones with back strain.

We worked in all weather except snow. We couldn't see the rocks in a snowstorm. But if it rained, we soldiered on, with special waterproof paper that didn't turn to pulp when it became soaked. Every day we spent ten or more hours exposed to the weather, alone in the wilderness, without seeing another human face.

Pickups started around six. An hour before, we would start to look for a spot where Chopper Mike could get in. If you were in a forest or thick brush, you needed a clearing. If there wasn't one within an hour's hike, you would have to make one yourself. We carried hatchets for that.

If you were on a mountain, you would look for a flat spot, or at least flat enough for the pilot to set down the helicopter skids. Chopper Mike could land on one skid hovering sideways against a mountain while the mapper climbed along the skid, careful not to upset the balance. Our pilot could even do a toe-hold, facing into the mountain. To get in, the passenger had to inch along the narrow skid partially suspended in air. This was a dangerous maneuver carrying a heavy pack, with the wind from the mountain and rotor blades gusting. If the person slipped, it could unbalance the chopper and might cause it to crash. If you were forced into this kind of retrieval, you were well aware that any mistake on your part could jeopardize the safety of everyone onboard.

With your pickup spot ready, you listened for the droning sound. When you heard it, you pulled out your radio and called the pilot in, describing your position.

"I'm at your three o'clock, low, halfway down the ridge."

Once you climbed into the flying glass egg, it was your job to help find the next person on the pickup list, looking for a tiny speck on the ground waving a dot of fluorescent orange plastic against a green background.

Flying back to camp I was amazed all over again, every single time, by how few seconds it took to fly over the traverse below that had taken me all day to walk.

The long day was not over yet. Drenched in mosquito repellent and sweat, we sorted our samples and plotted our data onto the map in the work tent. We coded the rock types by color and watched each day as the big master map grew—more data, more stations, more colors.

Once our data was plotted, if we had the energy, we might go down to the creek and wash out our socks or anything else. But most nights we didn't have time for that. Besides, clothes weren't likely to dry overnight, and putting on wet clothes was worse than wearing them dirty.

Dinner was the best part of the day. We ate plates full of Liz's fine cooking and swapped stories about the rocks, the animals we encountered, or the tricky landings Chopper Mike had pulled off.

Some days there were injuries or close calls due to rock slides or stream crossings. There was no shortage of things that could get you out here.

And there were the bears. Always their presence was seen and heard—the steaming lumps they left behind, the broken branches, or that terrifying sound of heavy thrashing in the bush that made you stop everything, even your own breathing, to listen in hope that the sound was receding. And usually it did. I tied a small bell to my pack that jingled as I walked, sending a message: *Strange human presence approaching. Stay away!* Most bears heeded the warning, content to avoid a human encounter. But not all of them.

Two weeks into the Livengood job I heard a thumping in the brush. I looked back and saw a black bear crashing through the trees. I kept moving to make sure it wouldn't follow me. But it was.

I went on, and so did the bear, closing the distance. Its intentions were clear—this bear was determined to force a confrontation.

There was no one around, nobody answering the radio, and nowhere to escape. I was surrounded by trees but this bear could climb them faster than I could. My worst nightmare was about to come true.

When it was so close that I could see the uneven patches in its fur, I turned to face it square on and drew my gun from my hip holster. The .44 snub-nosed revolver could fire six bullets, but it was loaded with four. I kept the first two chambers empty so that if the trigger snagged in the brush, it wouldn't discharge accidentally and put a bullet into my leg. As the bear kept coming, I loaded the two empty chambers, giving me a full six rounds. *Aim for the head.*

Suddenly I heard a roar overhead. The bear and I looked up at the same time. Our helicopter appeared over the ridge, coming in fast. Usually I heard the helicopter approach, sometimes from miles away. But if the wind was just right, it could surprise me. Right then, this was the best surprise ever.

I saw a flat spot off to the right and headed for it. I knew Chopper Mike saw it, too. I boarded in the back and the chopper muscled up before I even locked the door. As we lifted up and away, the bear tilted its head, a puzzled look on its face.

Inside the chopper, Mike apologized. Apparently his radio was malfunctioning. It could receive but not transmit. He *had* heard me, but wasn't able to let me know he was on the way.

This would have made a good story at dinner, if I had cared to tell it. Chopper Mike warned the others and that was enough. I had no need to relive the encounter. When the sun broke the next morning I would head out to those same hills again, with that bear still out there, more curious than ever.

After weeks spent this way, each day a banquet of new vistas, each night feeling exhausted to the edge of endurance, it was time to take down the camp. Everything had to be dismantled, repacked, and bundled into loads. The ground would be left as we found it. Packing up was always harder than moving in because every single thing was absolutely filthy by the end of the job.

Breaking down that Livengood tent city was a monumental operation. My first task was to take apart the cook tent. I packed away the dishes and what was left of the food, then took a crow-bar and ripped the nails out of the boards that had formed the shelves for Liz's kitchen. With the lumber and supplies all sorted into piles in the sling, I got down on my knees to roll up the canvas "carpet" that made up the floor.

As I peeled back a corner, the ground underneath moved. What was this? I leaned in for a better look. Big mistake. The dark ground below the canvas wasn't just moving; it was *writhing* with mice—hundreds of them, possibly thousands, in a solid breathing mass breeding and cavorting and dying down there with mousey abandon. They had been there all the time, right under our feet.

I got out of there as fast as I could, heading in the only direction I could think of—away.

"Where are you going?" the boss asked. "What about the cook tent?"

I had never shied away from a duty before. Nobody walked off on the job or talked back to Dr. Smith. But there was no power on earth that could have made me go back there.

Without stopping, or looking back, I said, "I am not dealing with the gray mouse family."

Dr. Smith's jaw dropped as he watched me go. I figured I was in trouble for sure. But he wasn't upset. He thought it was the funniest joke of the summer, something that he never allowed me to forget. Me, that gritty girl who refused to complain, who hauled as much as the guys, who carried my "Dirty Mary" gun tucked under my vest, so bad they could drop me in anywhere to do any job, to face anything.

Anything but a bunch of mice.

26.

⤳ Endless Summer ⤳

AFTER THE LIVENGOOD PROJECT, I joined another crew in the western Alaska Range just south of McGrath. Jeff Kline was running the project with Tom Bundtzen, a geologist who would get so engrossed thinking about rocks that he forgot the time, forgot to bring home the milk, and sometimes forgot to go home at all.

It was Jeff's job to coordinate and organize the McGrath crew. Unfortunately, organization wasn't Jeff's strong point. His camp management style was a lot like his office organization—complete chaos. Finding anything hidden in there was a challenge, even for Jeff. There were times he couldn't even read his own writing. He would show me his field notes, pages of horrible squiggles, and ask, "Hey, what do you think this says?"

With the low-key McGrath project following on the heels of the Livengood extravaganza, Jeff watched with growing annoyance as his project garnered unwelcome comparisons to the military precision of the biggest operation ever orchestrated by the Alaska Geological Survey.

Jeff boasted that the McGrath project was going to be done the *real* way, with few amenities and a small crew. He insisted that this way was best. As far as I was concerned, there was no "best" way. Exploration is hard work no matter how you slice it. Given the conditions we had to put up with, it was a small miracle if the work got done at all.

When I flew out to McGrath, Dr. Smith came too, but not to run the project. He would just be part of the crew.

Jeff worried that Dr. Smith would steal his thunder. I told Jeff there wouldn't be a problem, but he wasn't convinced. Jeff was one of the few people I ever met who worried more than me. When we got to McGrath, Dr. Smith took his turn at the map like everyone else, no drama at all.

The mountains at McGrath were more rugged than the Livengood terrain. This made it easier to see the rocks because they were more exposed. This also meant we had to do more rock climbing with those massive packs on our backs. And it meant that we had more than the usual amount of dangerous pickups with the chopper balanced precariously against a steep mountainside.

Whenever someone experienced a risky retrieval, an unspoken code kept us from talking about it while we were still in the air. No one said a word. But as soon as the helicopter touched down back at camp, everyone started talking at once. *Did you see the chopper dangling off that peak?* The geologist who had been forced to tight-rope across the hovering skid would smile, and we would congratulate him for cheating death once again. In doing so we were congratulating ourselves for being safe and well until the next morning when the helicopter flew us out once again.

~~~

By the time the McGrath project was completed, I had spent almost fifteen weeks in the bush. I thought I was finished for the summer. But one of our grad students, Gayle, needed help with her project because her assistant had quit two weeks before she could finish her work. Gayle was desperate for someone to go with her, so I agreed to help out.

We packed our gear into her truck, drove up the Steese Highway, and hiked in. For her project, charting the mineral content across a deposit, Gayle needed a continuous string of samples. This required carving a channel across the rock face with big hammers and collecting sections of rock chips and soil.

"Channel sampling" was dirty, dusty work. At the end of two weeks, we had dug the channel, bagged up the samples, and hauled them all back to the truck. We were coated in dust and grime.

When we got to town, Gayle wanted to stop at a grocery store. I thought we were too filthy to be seen in public. But after eating nothing but canned beans and rice, Gayle had a craving for fresh food and couldn't wait. She begged me to go with her. The thought of real food was too tempting to resist. I wiped off my glasses, big 1980s plastic frames that Elton John made so popular, and headed straight for the fresh produce section.

Of course people noticed us. How could they not? But most averted their eyes or moved away.

Then I realized this wasn't just any store. This was where I usually did my shopping. What was I thinking? How did I get talked into coming in here looking like this?

I hoped no one would recognize me. But it was too late. A boy about six stared at me with awe. I didn't think I knew him. But he continued to tug on his mother's sleeve and pointed at me standing there, coated in dust except for the one place I had managed to clean off, the lenses of my big round glasses.

"Look, Mommy," he said. "It's E.T!"

And so it was that in all of Fairbanks that year, the only alien sighting was me, in the grocery store right next to the grapes.

27.

~ A New Kind of Adventure ~

FOR OUR FIRST THANKSGIVING in the new house, Tom and I invited all of our friends for a feast of roast turkey, stuffing, sweet potatoes, and cranberry sauce made from berries I picked north of the campus. This secret berry patch was one of the perks of the summer spent mapping the Fairbanks district.

With our Thanksgiving dinner all cooked, Tom and I waited for our guests to arrive. We waited a long time. No one came, not a single person.

Apparently our friends had heard that Big Ron's mother was cooking and went to her place instead. Ron's mama was a fine cook who made the most delicious Welsh cakes. But when Ron's friends descended on her kitchen, uninvited, she served them breaded turkey sticks still cold from the fridge.

Our friends complained for days and were even more upset when they saw the sandwiches made with big hunks of turkey slathered with cranberry sauce that Tom and I took to work.

After that, we had no shortage of guests at our holiday table. One of our guests was Karen Clautice. She had worked with me at the Bureau of Mines, and later at the Alaska survey. Whenever she came over, Karen always left something behind, and I was constantly bringing back her dishes, mittens, or whatever else she had forgotten.

One Thanksgiving, she brought her baby son, Danny, who was so small that she carried him inside in his traveling "bed," a plastic laundry basket. When Karen got ready to go home, I checked the whole house for baby things, determined that she wasn't going to leave anything behind.

After the guests went home, Tom and I cleaned up the kitchen and I went outside to bring the dogs in for the night. There they were in the dog house all cuddled together, three sets of eyes peering out at me.

Three? We only had two dogs. The third dog was Sadie, Karen's blue-eyed husky. Karen had managed to leave something behind after all.

I had lost something, too—my appetite. I wasn't hungry the rest of the day and felt sick all the next morning.

When I bought a home pregnancy test, the blue stripe told me I was going to have a baby. Tom and I jumped up and down and told everyone in town. This was going to be a different kind of adventure.

By this time, Yvonne had taken a job in Wasilla near Anchorage, 230 miles south of Fairbanks. But I had a new friend, Sarah, who lived down the street. Her husband Ray had worked on one of Tom's crews. Two weeks later, she discovered that she was pregnant, too.

Sarah's husband was a skilled craftsman who had built their house, a sturdy log cabin with beautiful hand-carved furniture. Their dining-room table was a thick slab of burl mounted on top of a tree trunk, its roots reaching out and winding under the chairs as if it had grown there.

Inspired by Ray, Tom picked up some carpentry tricks that winter and made me exactly what I wanted for Christmas—my own dog sled. We had two dogs, Ginger, the collie-husky mutt, and our pure white Ruby, who was half wolf. Indoors, Ruby was a queen, gracefully lording over everything in sight, including my bunny slippers. Outdoors she heard the call of the wild and ran like the wind. When she got loose, I had to drive up and down the road calling out the one thing that brought my wolf-dog beast home:

"Yummies! Who wants their yummies?"

The little sled Tom built was just the right size to hitch up our two dogs and mush over to Sarah's house.

I had learned to run dogs from Shirley Liss, one of our geologists who was also a long-distance musher. With her perpetual smile, Shirley was known for her good nature and resourcefulness. She lived way out in the Goldstream Valley in a cabin that she built with her own two hands, surrounded by a dozen doghouses, each occupied by a big howling malamute you could hear for miles. The entire chorus of them was like a dog opera. Shirley knew each dog by its bark and could distinguish the different tones for different occasions. There was the dinner bark, demanding and throaty; the I-want-to-play bark that was light and breezy; and a low moaning howl she only heard once, moments before the Good Friday Earthquake in 1964.

On the weekends, Shirley ran her dog team through the Goldstream Valley. Once in a while she mushed to work, parking the dogs in the woods behind the office. She had made long-distance sled-dog runs with her big friendly malamutes, a breed known for endurance rather than speed. In the winter of 1983, when the Yukon Quest, a new long-distance sled-dog race was organized, she wanted to sign up. This race would be run one thousand miles (1,600 km) between Fairbanks and Whitehorse, Yukon Territory, Canada, in some of the coldest weather and roughest conditions in the world, including three mountain passes higher than 3,400 feet (1,000 m).

Shirley was eager to face the challenge but couldn't afford the three-hundred-dollar entry fee. This didn't seem right, that her dream of doing something so extraordinary might go unfulfilled because of the fee.

"I'll get you the money," I told her. "Everyone wants to see you in that race. People will be glad to donate to get you in."

When people learned I was collecting donations, they lined up to put their dollars into the hat. We had enough for the fee in less than a week. Shirley became the first woman to sign up for the first running of the Yukon Quest, a race that over the years became a huge international event attracting worldwide attention.

As Shirley prepared for the race that winter, I often went over to her little cabin and watched her train. She had a way of talking about her past mushing adventures that made me feel as if I had been there, too. One time she had been stranded in a blizzard near Nome. With her food running out and unable to see her hand at arm's length, she was saved by the tenacity and loyalty of her lead dog Sapphire, who led the team to safety.

As Shirley sewed dog harnesses, I learned to make them as well. I watched her assemble supplies for the race, including meals for the dogs. To pull the sled over the mountains, her dogs would need more protein than she could get in store-bought dog food. Her solution? She chopped up a dead horse, a friend's animal. When the horse died of natural causes, the owner loaded it into the back of his pickup truck, where it froze solid with the legs sticking up. I had seen this truck driving around—you could hardly miss it with a dead, upside-down horse in the back.

Once she received the donated carcass, she sawed the frozen horse into chunks and put the pieces—hair, bones, and all—into steel buckets on top of her woodstove and cooked it into a thick stew. Then she poured the stew outside onto the snow where it froze solid. She took the frozen mass and chopped it into meal-sized chunks about the size of popsicles. She called them "horsicles." Her dogs loved them.

I accompanied Shirley on her practice runs. The first time we went, I sat in the basket of the sled as it banged along, careening into trees and spilling me out on the steep turns. It wasn't much fun being battered against the sled's wooden frame. After that, we hooked up two sleds and I drove one of the teams.

Shirley didn't do anything by small measures. The first time I drove one of her sled teams, we went on a 50-mile (80 km) race to the winter retreat of Mary Shields, who had been one of the first women to run the Iditarod Trail Sled Dog Race. There was no road to her winter cabin. The only way to get there was to hike or mush through the miles of wilderness.

I found that the principles of driving a dog team were simple, involving only a handful of commands: gee (turn right), haw (turn left), and whoa (stop). Getting the dogs to obey was another matter, especially if they smelled a squirrel or a moose or anything else that caught their attention.

Once they got going, Shirley's big malamutes didn't like to stop, forcing me to use the brake. This was a piece of wood with metal teeth made from long, curved prongs. The brake was attached to the sled by a chain; to stop the sled, you would throw this brake onto the ground and stomp the teeth into the snow. Traveling at the speed of a running dog pack, this wasn't an easy maneuver.

My sledding adventure to Mary Shields' winter place was an unforgettable experience. After hours of racing headlong through snowy, pristine forests, we rounded a bend in the trail and came upon a group of exquisite log cabins laid out like a miniature town, all built with hand tools; there were no power lines out here. One cabin was her house, one was the sauna, and another stored her sleds; the one on the end was a workshop with a sanded pine floor that was cleaner than my kitchen table.

This annual race to Mary's wilderness get-away was not a serious sporting event but a jovial yearly gathering of mushers, with bonus

points awarded for silly things. You earned extra points for wearing
the most ridiculous hat, the ugliest coat, or for having the most dogs
on your team. The number of dogs was counted by the number of tails.
The year I mushed the "Mary Shields' Invitational," one musher cheated
to earn extra points. With the wind howling behind him, he burst into
the cabin, his beard frosted with snow, wearing a giant leather cord
necklace strung with tails he had collected throughout the year, severed
from dogs that had died.

"This was Josie," he said, holding one up, "my lead dog for five
years. Remember that time she pulled my team over the pass when
nobody could get through? Then, the next day she got loose and started
a fight with every dog on the team. What a dog! Shame about the cancer."

Out here in their element, those mushers were a gregarious
bunch. They made me feel welcome as they shared their stories of epic
journeys, the quirky personalities of their canine partners, and traded
news and gossip.

Later that winter, I volunteered to be part of Shirley's Yukon Quest
support crew, flying with the pilots who made a daily pass over the
route. In a small two-seater plane, we spotted the teams and counted
the tiny little dots in the snow far below to make sure all was well.
Several mushers found they couldn't handle the extreme cold and the
steep mountain passes, and were forced to quit. This race through
sub-arctic wilderness with few checkpoints was a lonely, self-reliant
journey. Just finishing the Yukon Quest would be a major achievement.
The race's unofficial motto said it all: "Survive first, race second."

As the mushers headed away from Fairbanks, Shirley's big malamute
dogs were not in the forefront of the pack, but she didn't give up.

By the time Shirley reached the Yukon River about two weeks
later, a sudden warm spell was melting the snow at the finish line in
Whitehorse, so race officials decided to end the race in the Canadian
village of Carmacks. As Shirley neared the finish line, I drove ahead
with a friend, Mary Spilde, to be on hand for Shirley's proud moment.
And what a moment it was. Although it was late at night when her team
slid over the finish line, a small crowd had gathered with race officials,
locals, and kids with dogs all cheering her on. Every team behind her
had dropped out, and Shirley was awarded the Red Lantern Award for
finishing last.

That night, Shirley staked her dogs outside in a snowy field with beds of straw while the good people of Carmacks put the three of us up in their recreation hall. We laid out our sleeping bags on the wooden slat benches in the women's changing room, ripe with the universal odor of locker rooms everywhere as Shirley wound down from her trip. We listened with rapt attention well into the morning hours as she shared the details that were so fresh on her mind. Her big malamutes were not the fastest dogs on the trail, but in an ice storm she had used them to help pull weaker teams in trouble up over one of the passes. In a sport where the frontrunners often trick each other or psych out their competitors, Shirley ran a different sort of quest.

I felt honored and awe-struck to be part of this magic moment of history, even if only vicariously as Shirley shared her stories and I watched her transform before me from the world of sub-arctic survival back into the world of mankind.

~

With the stout little sled Tom built for me, I could hook up my two-dog team any time I wanted and go on my own modest dog-sled jaunts. The only problem was that my sled didn't have a brake. To stop it, I dragged my foot. With only two dogs pulling, that usually worked on flat ground or on an uphill slope. But Sarah's house was downhill all the way. Sarah would hear my dogs barking and run out to see me sliding down the road as my sled boards scraped against the ice.

Going downhill, there was no controlling Ruby, our white alpha wolf dog. All I could do was hang on for dear life until she got tired enough to slow down.

"I'll be back!" I would call out to Sarah as we blasted down the hill. Sarah would laugh and wave, then go back inside to put on the kettle, knowing from experience how long it would be until Ruby decided she'd had enough exercise.

That winter, Sarah and I shopped for baby clothes and often talked long into the night about children and motherhood and how things were going to change. We could hardly wait for our babies to come.

We weren't the only ones. In 1983, three other women at the state survey, including Kristin Kline and John Dillon's wife, Mary Morman, a water chemist, became pregnant, too.

We formed the "preggy club," meeting to discuss health care and nutrition and to treat our bodies to special exercises—at least that was the plan. At the first meeting, after a few half-hearted arm stretches, we dove into the snack tray and obliterated every crumb of the crackers and high-calorie cheese. So much for our good intentions.

As the winter wore on and we grew bigger every week, Sarah and I scoured the shops for baby things. We shuffled around town like a pair of old ladies, careful not to fall on the ice and hurt the tiny people that were growing inside us.

As spring approached, we were swollen up like balloons. Then, one night, I woke up with my stomach in somersaults and climbed down from the loft into the kitchen.

Tom heard me riffling around in the refrigerator.

"What are you doing?" he called down.

"I'm packing."

"Packing what?"

"Your breakfast." I said. "It's time to go to the hospital."

He jumped out of bed, got the car started, and off we went.

"It's too bumpy," I said during a contraction. "Slow down."

He slowed down to a crawl. When the contraction was over, I yelled out, "Go faster! We've got to get there!"

"Really?" he said. "You want me to go fast?"

"The faster the better."

"Great!" he said, flooring the gas. "Maybe we'll get stopped. I have always wanted to say, 'But officer, my wife is having a baby!'"

He happily drove like a madman, but no one noticed or cared at four in the morning.

At the hospital, in between contractions, we phoned our families on the East Coast, telling them the good news.

"Oh yes, I'm in labor. Right... *now!*"

The fun didn't last long. Soon the contractions became more frequent, and racked my body with pain. Now it was work, but the baby wouldn't come.

The night shift nurses left, and the day shift arrived. Still, no baby. The ordeal went on and on and on. Having grown up on a farm, I was no stranger to hard physical labor, but this was light years beyond anything I had ever come up against for sheer, unending, unabated agony. And still, no end was in sight.

The night nurses came back, wondering why I was still in contractions three shifts later. It gave me no comfort that the doctor didn't understand, either.

Desperately trying to be helpful, Tom brought me some ice chips. As if a cup of ice would make up for getting me in this predicament. After fifteen hours of my guts trying to rip themselves apart, my response was not charitable.

"I don't want that damn ice, I want this baby out. Get me a C-section. Now!"

The doctor explained it was too late for a Caesarean birth. The baby was stuck in the birth canal. One way or another, it was going to have to come out between my legs, even though there wasn't nearly enough room.

The ordeal went on until 6 a.m. the next morning. Then my contractions stopped. I had used all my energy, all my reserves, and my body could do nothing more than prepare to shut down.

If I wasn't at a hospital conveniently loaded with drugs, it would have been all over. The doctor pumped me with Pitocin, a pituitary hormone extract that forces labor contractions, and then brought out a syringe as long as her forearm with the dreaded giant needle to apply a saddle block for anesthesia. One wrong move with that needle and I would be paralyzed for life. Before that day, the thought of this procedure had made me shudder. Now I could hardly wait for that wicked needle to be rammed up my spine.

After the procedure, the doctor brought out a pair of forceps so large they looked as if they had come from a blacksmith. The doc jammed them into places I wouldn't have believed they would fit, all mercifully without any feeling at all thanks to my new best friend, Mister Needle.

Finally, there was my baby girl, with huge wondering eyes, curved welts on her cheeks from the forceps, and a full head of wet curls the same color as my hair—the exact same chestnut-red shade.

They wrapped her up and said not to worry, she was safely out and they would bring her back soon. They sent Tom home to get some sleep. Alone in my room, I drifted off, glad it was over, knowing that when I woke up, my baby would be there beside me.

Sometime in the dark hours before morning, I was prodded awake—no baby in sight—and presented with a stack of documents.

"Sign these," someone said. "Disclaimers."

I was told that my baby had to be airlifted to Seattle for tests that could kill her. I had to sign my name here, and here, and here, to release everyone from lawsuits in case my little girl died from the blue dye they would inject into her heart.

None of this made any sense.

"I need to see her," I said. "They said they would bring her right back. They said she was fine."

"Your baby is not fine," said a nurse. "Anyone with a stethoscope and ears would know that your baby's heart is most certainly not fine."

I signed the papers and sat there with the phone in my lap. But I didn't call Tom, not yet. He needed those few hours of sleep because soon he would be rushed to Seattle with the baby. I couldn't do it. They wouldn't allow me to go. I had lost too much blood.

By then, two other new mothers had joined me in the hospital room, cuddling their healthy bundles of joy while I lay there alone with my horrible secret. I listened to them cooing over their babies and phoning their friends until I couldn't stand it anymore. I slipped out of the bed to go find my baby.

The next thing I knew, nurses were pulling me up from the cold floor. I had passed out.

Time seemed to collapse as I spent days in hospitals feeling numb, waiting for news. Tessa's little heart stopped twice as my baby lay in her daddy's lap in a rocking chair at an intensive-care unit in Seattle. But the doctors got it beating again with electric shocks.

After two weeks, knowing every moment could have been her last, the doctors cleared her to leave the hospital. Tom and I brought our baby girl home. She liked the window at the top of the house that filled the walls with colored rays of light. She stared at the big white dog with the eraser-pink nose.

But she liked the outdoors best, just like me. With her big eyes, she looked up at those tall trees that sheltered our house as she listened to the musical sound of the wind. She loved that sound, but not for long. A week later she was back in the hospital.

The nurses averted their eyes when they saw me.

"Try not to blame yourself," said one nurse. I suppose she meant to be helpful but this made me angry that on top of everything else she had the nerve to try to introduce guilt into the equation.

Sarah, who had given birth a week after me and gone home with a healthy boy, no longer visited. She didn't even call.

A month later, they operated on Tessa. The surgery to repair my baby's tiny heart, scheduled for two hours, took more than six. Finally the doctor came out and said it was over—a complete success. They were closing her chest. My baby would live!

I went downstairs to force myself to eat for the first time that day. Half a yoghurt later, I went back up to the waiting room. But Tom looked different. His smile was gone.

As the surgeons were sewing up the hole in Tessa's little chest, her heart gave up. It just stopped. Nothing they did could bring it back this time. It had been too stressed for too long.

Time compressed again.

They burned her in an oven and she never got to wear her ruffled blue dress with the powder pink bow.

The service was held in the trees on a hill above the college. Everyone came—everyone but Sarah. She was too busy with her own life, with her own child, and didn't want to be reminded of mine.

Soon after, Sarah and her husband packed what they could fit into their truck and drove away to California. They had no jobs there, no friends, and no home. They didn't even wait to sell their log house. Sarah had decided it was time to leave Fairbanks. It was time to leave me. So I lost my daughter and my friend at the same time.

28.

✸ Frontier Lottery ✸

Y PARENTS FLEW UP FOR THE BURIAL. Back then, they were in the prime of their lives, vigorous and strong. Yet, when they got off the plane, they looked more haggard than I had ever seen them before (or since). As brand-new grandparents, losing their only grandchild was a soul-crushing "first" loss for them, too.

Father Jim performed the service even though we were not Catholic. After Jeff's complicated wedding, many of us at the Alaska survey called on Father Jim for our spiritual needs. For more than a decade, the priest was our go-to man for weddings, baptisms, and the sad occasions such as this. After the burial service, Tom and I got out of our funeral clothes and drove my parents north on the Steese Highway to the Circle Hot Springs Resort. The lodge was a grand old three-story hotel, surrounded by a smattering of log cabins and out buildings and a swimming pool fed by the hot springs.

A few months before, I had been a winner in the state's annual land lottery, and the state sent me the deed for four acres of land near the hot springs. Land lotteries were a product of the old west as a means to distribute remote land fairly. As the last frontier state, Alaska was still holding these land lotteries. I had entered my name for this plot and won the right to buy it for four hundred dollars an acre. Even one hundred fifty miles (240 km) from town, the price seemed to be a bargain.

My land was a mile from the hot springs. At that time, you could swim at the lodge in an outdoor pool of sulfuric water that was as hot as soup. It smelled like rotten eggs and oxidized any silver jewelry you were wearing into a charcoal black, but the steamy temperature was divine. The hot springs were not far from where I had mapped the evaporites for the Bureau of Mines. Later, Tom and I had stayed at the lodge during a claim-staking job. I was particularly fond of the region even though I knew there were problems near the hot springs with radioactive radon gas. This made sense; the hot water had to come from somewhere.

My father, who still harbored his dream of moving out west, was thrilled when I won the land lottery and immediately drafted plans to build a getaway cabin. At the time I didn't know he would get his first look at the land on the day of his first grandchild's burial.

We went up to the hot springs in my brown Landcruiser and checked into the lodge. After consulting the map the state land office sent me, we drove off to find Red Fox Road. We found the turnoff, but it wasn't a road; it was an overgrown rut through a swamp. But lack of roads had never stopped us before so we drove right in. In years of off-roading, my Landcruiser had never gotten stuck. That beast had crossed streams and crashed through the brush like a tank. But as we turned onto this "road," my rig was about to meet its match.

Three hundred yards in, we began to sink. We engaged the four-wheel drive and charged ahead a little farther through the deep mud. Soon we were no longer merely stuck; we were four-wheel-drive stuck.

The big wheels were buried in muck half-way up the hub caps. Then we saw something ominous—a black cloud was heading our way. It was a flying maelstrom of mosquitoes. In no time they were on us, ravenous for our blood, a cloud of tiny vampires coating us like a black paste. It wasn't just skin they attacked. They invaded our ears and went up our noses. With every breath, we coughed and spit out mouthfuls of bugs. By this time, I had spent many summers in the bush, fighting off swarms of flying blood-suckers, but this swarm was worse than anything I'd ever seen. Years before, I had read in Peter Freuchen's *Famous Book of the Eskimos* that at times mosquitoes can literally drive a reindeer insane. I was skeptical then but became a believer that day on Red Fox Road.

With the Landcruiser stuck, we hiked half a mile in to the property, a small mound of scrub brush and cottonwood trees. Without a road, there was no access to power or water or anything else. The view, swamp in every direction, didn't hold our attention for long through the dense clouds of mosquitoes. We paused long enough to snap a quick photo before making a hasty retreat to the Landcruiser.

So much for my father's vacation land dream.

After a few moments of shelter inside the swamped vehicle, we made a mad dash back to the lodge. It took one of the state's big snowplows to pull the Landcruiser back out to the road.

We never built a cabin on that land, but I still have the deed, proclaiming that I am a frontier land baron, even if it is just a slab of radioactive arctic swamp.

Back in Fairbanks, I folded away the empty crib to make room for my parents and their sleeping bags on the floor. We made small talk, trying to dance around the sadness that words could not ease.

My dad put a new roof on our A-frame. He was glad to be busy. In the meantime, I showed my mother the arctic treasures I had collected, each one a story from my travels. There was a pair of fossilized walrus ivory earrings I bought from a native boy in the village of Buckland, a few hundred miles from Nome. Buckland was one of the most isolated places I had ever seen—no roads, just a dirt airstrip. Bush planes were the only way to get in and out of this village unless you waited for winter and mushed a dog team to Nome.

I showed my mother a pair of mukluks made of reindeer skin that I bought in a village near the Canadian border. To make the curved parts of the boot, the women worked the hides with their teeth, chewing the hide into shape. The locals could tell who made the boots by the pattern of teeth marks in the leather.

In a village on the Kuskokwim River delta in southwest Alaska, I bought a grass basket made the traditional way, the grass woven so tightly that the basket could hold water. The Eskimos developed this form of extreme weaving to make vessels for cooking. In treeless areas, the only materials available were the weeds and grass.

It was hard to imagine cooking food in a straw basket, but those early natives found a way. First, they would fill the straw basket with water and raw meat. Then they would start a fire and heat rocks in it. When the rocks were hot, they would drop them into the basket until the water reached the boiling point, cooking the meat.

I had purchased my basket from a village woman with quick, gnarled fingers and a leathery smile. She knew all about cooking food the old way. Out in her little cabin, she didn't get many visitors. Most of her baskets were sold at the World Eskimo-Indian Olympics in

Fairbanks, where natives from Alaska and Canada gathered once a year to compete in traditional events. One event called the "ear pull" tested the competitor's endurance for pain. This was a hugely popular event—as a spectator sport. But it was hard for me to enjoy the sight of young men bearing the pain of having their ears pulled. As a child, my brother had his ear ripped off by one of our horses, and I knew just how easy it was to remove one. Luckily, with a hospital nearby, ears are relatively easy to sew back on.

I went to the games as often as I could. My favorite sport was the blanket toss. For this event, someone is hurled high into the air on a trampoline made of a large patchwork of animal hides. Instead of a frame, the blanket is held by a circle of people all around the edge. The blanket toss originally was a way to spot game on the flat, treeless arctic plain—the higher you bounced, the better your chances for a successful hunt.

While watching the blanket toss, I was struck by the different ways the athletes had devised to gain height. Some flapped their hands, some churned their legs, and some pumped their arms. Others arched their backs and kept their arms still as their bodies rocketed up. It was stunning to see how high they could go, powered by nothing but animal hides and human ingenuity.

At the native craft tables, I watched one sculptor from the arctic coast carve a slit into a piece of wood to make goggles—traditional "sun glasses." From another young craftsman who came from western Alaska, I bought a round-edged knife with a bone handle shaped like a bear. This was an ulu, traditionally a woman's knife with a wide curved blade meant for chopping, not stabbing. Knives with sharp points traditionally were reserved for men. The folklore maintained that a woman's touch could rob a man's knife of its power and strength. Because a village was dependent on the food that it hunted, the penalty in some villages for a woman who touched a man's knife was death.

Of all the pieces in my collection, the one that held the place of pride in my home was the beaded birch cradle with moose leather straps, just right for carrying on the back. After so many seasons of packing gear, I knew about carrying my worldly belongings on my back and couldn't wait until I had the ultimate treasure to place inside it.

Now the cradle sat on a shelf, gathering dust, never to carry a newborn child.

29.

~ The Chuilnuks ~

*A*FTER TWO WEEKS, MY PARENTS WENT HOME to Syracuse and I went back to work. I hadn't planned to get into the field that summer. I was supposed to take maternity leave. But with everyone out in the camps, the office was a dead zone, as empty as my heart.

I needed to get into the field.

The big project that season was run by John Decker, a fast-talking card shark who had met his wife Steffany at a poker game. Steffany, who worked in our office coloring maps, had been a member in the preggy club. She, Kristin Kline, and Mary Morman had all delivered fine baby boys.

I had never worked for Decker before and wasn't sure how he would react to my request to be on his team. So soon after childbirth, I wasn't in top field-worthy shape. My stitches hadn't yet healed.

"I would like to go out on your field project," I told him.

"You just had a baby."

"I don't have one now. I need to get out there."

He went silent a moment and frowned. I thought he was trying to figure out how to turn me down politely. Then he spoke.

"After watching what my wife went through with childbirth," he said, "anyone who can handle that can be on my crew."

A few days later, I was on my way. Eight of us in the crew were on a commercial flight to Aniak. For most of the flight, the windows were cloaked in clouds.

Abruptly the plane banked sharply, throwing us sideways. On the down-wing side, I was surprised that the color that suddenly filled my window was wrong. The green of grass was so close I could see the individual blades as the wing nearly scraped the ground. Somehow we had come out of the clouds so low that we missed crashing by inches.

As the passengers lurched in their seats I saw their faces. The people on the up-side of the plane saw only blue sky out their windows. They were confused and didn't understand what the problem was.

On my side of the plane, the passengers saw what I had seen, and their faces were flushed with shock.

Strangely enough, I wasn't afraid. After Tessa's death, it was a while before I could feel physical pain. My pain centers were still numb. As I watched the grass blowing in our exhaust, I realized that my emotional receptors and fear instinct had been dampened as well.

I knew something else—that my baby Tessa was still around, that her spirit had not yet departed because I saw her out of the corner of my eye—a flash of her face peering at me, then disappearing just as I turned. Those first few weeks I saw her often, always outside—she loved the outdoors—behind rocks and gnarled trees and in the swirling foam of the Nenana River on the white-water raft trip that Tom and I took for a diversion. I knew she was not far. I knew that if the plane had crashed, Tessa would have been there to meet me.

But the plane didn't crash. After that, I didn't see her again. She no longer waited for me, and I had to get on with my life.

From the Aniak air strip, we went straight to the chopper that took us to our base camp, about thirty miles (48 km) away. One tent had been set up along the lip of a high lake surrounded by the ice-cream-cone peaks of the Chuilnuk Mountains. Across the water, the rocky spires were so perfectly mirrored in the lake that it was hard to distinguish the mountains from the reflection.

We were greeted by Mark Robinson, a geologist who had come ahead to start setting up the camp.

"When you get tired of that view," he said, "we'll change the slide." He was right; the view didn't look real. It looked like a travel poster.

I was assigned to accompany John Reiker, our resident mathematician, as the helicopter took him around to collect gravity readings. With his wild frizzled hair, and glasses that magnified his eyes to fill up the entire frame, he looked every bit the part of a scientist collecting data for his third-order derivative gravitational field modeling, or something to that effect. We were told he was a genius.

That may have been true, but he couldn't navigate his way out of a paper bag or find himself on a map. For that, he had me.

The helicopter would drop us in, Reiker would position his gravimeter for a reading, and I would plot the location on the map. Then we would fly off to the next spot among those jagged peaks to take another reading.

This was easy work. We didn't climb up or down, hike anywhere, or carry gear on our backs. It was all the scenery and camaraderie of field work without any of the slog.

It was too easy. After three days of this, I asked Decker to put me back out mapping rocks. I needed something more than baby-sitting the whiz kid to drive the demons from my mind.

Fitted out for winter claim staking on one of Karl Hanneman's crews. We had to be careful around the helicopter's rotor blades.

Tom bagging a field sample in the Kugarouk Mountains.

Getting ready to ski down a mountain near Circle after a claim-staking job. I had not yet done any downhill skiing, so I used a sled.

*O*ur "kozy cabin" on Chena Ridge near Fairbanks.

*T*he inside of the house we bought, an A-frame.

I used an auger to hand-drill the depth of evaporite deposits in the Circle flats. The deposits turned out to be disappointingly thin.

*G*etting into the chopper
at the Livengood camp.

I'm hard at work
measuring rock.

*Y*vonne Grace, left, and me on a rocky hillside north of Anchorage.

*V*iew from the top in the White Mountains.

$\mathcal{R}$uby, our wolf dog, and me, about to go sledding.

$\mathcal{E}$very house should have one—a white wolf dog guarding your bunny slippers.

$\mathcal{M}$y swamp lottery land on Red Fox Road. At $400 an acre, this land was a bargain, if you could get there.

*M*y go-anywhere jeep got stuck on the "road" to my swamp land. Tom's attempt to extract the jeep proved futile. A state snow plow pulled us out.

*S*etting up the Chuilnuk camp near Aniak.

*T*he outrageous view from our camp site of the Chuilnuk Mountains.

Karen Clautice and me dressed as dance-hall girls for the Miner's Ball. One of the guys in the office thought he was paying us a compliment when he said, "You don't make such bad-looking whores."

I was "Miss April" in the 1995 calendar from the Juneau branch of the Alaska Miners Association.

The first and last fish I caught in Alaska was a seventy-four-pound king salmon from the Kenai River.

Tom and me with our girls on the Oregon Coast in 1990. Amy, who was three, had arrived from Thailand a few months before. Yvonne was six.

*M*e with our girls.

*T*om and me.

30.

✒ Kicking Down Doors ✒

$\mathcal{I}$ RETURNED FROM ANIAK IN LATE AUGUST as the last blooms of magenta fireweed were turning to straw. Looking ahead to the winter, I realized I needed something new to move myself forward instead of getting lost in the past. I still hadn't returned to the physical shape I had been in before getting pregnant, and found a lunch-time karate class that might fit the bill. I had taken some martial arts way back in college. This seemed like a good time to pick it up again.

The class was taught by Kit Hale, one of the few women who had risen to black-belt level under the formidable Charles Scott, a seventh-degree grand master and the much-admired vice principal of a local high school. Kit rented space to teach her classes in the master's dojo located in a cellar under the bakery downtown.

This cellar workout room was a dark and stuffy hole in the ground with a light bulb dangling from a crossbeam and not much else. The dirt floor, not entirely level, was covered by pieces of mildewed carpet. There were no windows, no bathroom, and no showers or sinks. Every time I climbed down the creaky wooden steps into that cellar, I was met by the overwhelming smell of stale sweat mixed with the bakery's sourdough yeast.

Without changing rooms, the men had to get into their karate outfits behind a tarp strung up on the punching bag while the women used the boiler room. We hung our clothes high up on the furnace pipes. Anything left on the ground would end up crawling with silverfish, a blind wiggling insect that likes to burrow into clothing and can live up to a year without eating. I was so glad when Kit eventually opened a new studio in a proper building with clean walls and fresh paint.

After a while, I started to rise through the ranks. With my baby gone, there was a hole inside me that burned like a fire pit, and karate was the only place it would vent.

Kit was an excellent teacher, imparting what she knew about focusing the power within and delivering it where you aimed. But one thing that she couldn't do was to remember her keys.

The first time Kit realized she hadn't brought her studio keys, we all stood outside facing the locked door. I thought we were done for the day. But Kit said, "All right people. It's time for some *kick drills!*" Then she slammed her foot through the door.

Her husband, a carpenter, was not pleased.

The next time Kit forgot her keys, she told me it was my turn to do the honors. I couldn't believe it. It is one thing to practice kicking into the air, but a different thing entirely to smash through an exterior door built to withstand a Fairbanks winter. How could my bare foot break through? I didn't think I could do it, but I gave it a try. On my first attempt, the door would not yield. On the second, I busted through. It was sobering to learn I could do this.

Along with training the body, karate required new ways of thinking and I learned two important things about kicking through doors. The first rule is that you must not aim for the door; you aim beyond it. Otherwise, you have no chance of breaking through. The second thing I discovered is that when you smash through the door, the door takes the blow and you hardly feel the impact. However, if you don't make it through, your body absorbs the impact. This hurts, and you could be injured. In other words, *go through or else*, which is a powerful incentive to not hold anything back.

Kit was good teaching children. In one class, a little boy was punched in the face accidentally and lost a tooth. His gums squirted blood like a fountain. Kit stopped the bleeding, found the tooth, iced the boy's mouth, and then explained to the class about the ninja tooth fairy that leaves a special gift for children who lose teeth in karate class. Kit conferred with the parents, and the next morning the little boy was delighted to find a tin throwing star under his pillow, as shiny as Bruce Lee's.

Kit was the only martial artist I ever met who could work with toddlers. If they could walk, no matter how unsteadily, she could get them punching and kicking red balloons across the room. At karate tournaments, her toddler team brought down the house, performing to the tune of Whitney Houston's song, *we are the world* (punch, punch); *we are the children* (kick, kick). There was not a single adult in the crowd who wasn't moved by that sight.

I didn't need inspiration. I continued to train, attacking the fire pit inside me with all that I had.

Along with my job at the Alaska Geological Survey, I started teaching geology correspondence classes for the university. Most of my students were teachers who worked in the bush and wanted a science class to freshen their knowledge. This was part-time work that I could fit in on the weekends.

With my job, part-time teaching, and karate, I should have been busy enough. But when a big statewide mining conference was scheduled for Fairbanks in the spring of 1985, I volunteered to serve on the organizing committee. About a dozen people agreed to serve on the committee, but only two of us showed up at the first meeting, and I found myself sitting at a very large table across from Kathy Goff.

Kathy and I lined up a program, booked the speakers, and arranged to get those people to the conference. We moderated the sessions, making sure all the speakers had the audio-visual equipment they required, and then threw a big chili feed to thank them for coming. On the last night of the conference, we helped host a miner's ball with period costumes from the gold-rush days. Afterward, we published a book reporting on the proceedings. It was an insane amount of work.

Meanwhile, our office faced budget cuts and the possibility of layoffs. This was unthinkable. Our branch of the state survey was more than a team. Out in the field, we lived together like a family. With all those summers spent in tent camps, with no walls between us, we got to know everyone's habits—who snored, who sulked when it rained, and who played guitar badly. We knew about everyone's lives, their fears, and their bad jokes.

Even back in town, we had few secrets. One day Jeff slipped out of the office for an appointment. He went at noon, thinking no one would notice. By the time he returned at one o'clock, there was a card on his desk gleefully signed by everyone on staff that read: "Congratulations on your vasectomy!"

When you know people that well, you can't bear to see them expelled from "the family."

John Dillon had been the union representative when I joined the Alaska survey. Later, he asked me to take the job. It wasn't much work, he said, just an annual meeting, so I agreed. It was no big deal until layoffs appeared on the horizon.

When I went to the union with our concerns, the union officials were indifferent. Why should they care? As they told me, their own paychecks were not at risk.

I couldn't bear to allow this to happen so I cooked up a plan with another insurgent, Dr. Smith. What if our entire office agreed to a pay cut? Could we avoid layoffs?

We put it to a vote. When three-quarters of our people agreed to accept pay cuts to avoid losing members of staff, I called a reporter. When the story hit the news, the union officials were livid. How dare we take our destiny in our own hands? They postured and shouted and threatened to kick me out of the union.

I met with the union president.

"You know this is wrong," I told him. "One of those geologists slated for layoff was on the team that discovered Prudhoe Bay. Without him, we wouldn't have that pipeline. The state finances would still be in the toilet, and your job wouldn't exist."

"We have enough oil," the union president told me. "That's all in the past. What we need now is more transportation—more roads that go nowhere, and people to maintain them. I work for the Department of Transportation, and that's where my pay hikes come from."

It was an appalling example of short-sighted greed. I needed a larger platform to present our case. So when a seat opened up on the Fairbanks North Star Borough Assembly, I decided to run for election. I filmed my own TV commercials, participated in debates, and met with various interest groups.

During this time I was working full-time for the Alaska survey, organizing a statewide conference, competing on the karate circuit, fighting the union, and running for office. What was I thinking?

I hardly saw Tom at all. He put in long hours, too, taking on new responsibilities as Nerco grew into a statewide leader in the industry. As for me, my life was a barely controlled chaos. When I left the house each morning, I packed two or three changes of clothes for all the roles I would have to play that day.

It would be crazy to take on anything else.

However, when the Fairbanks Symphony Orchestra announced it was looking for a guest conductor for the spring concert, who raised their hand? That would be me.

I had played the violin in orchestra throughout my high school years, but not at symphony level. I had never conducted either, a task that required reading the parts for every instrument simultaneously and bringing them all in at exactly the right time. My first rehearsal with the symphony was a trial by fire as I discovered the horrible mishmash of sounds that come out when the conductor gets it wrong.

The second rehearsal was better. By the night of the performance, we were making real music. The audience cheered as I took my bows in my floor-length dress and big bouffant hair. I had done it!

As the throngs of people crowded around to shake my hand, someone said, "And congratulations on your poem winning second place in the radio contest."

I smiled, not from joy but to mask my confusion.

Poem? What radio contest?

Then he quoted some of the verses, and they sounded vaguely familiar. A distant memory came back. Yes, I had seen something like that scribbled on a page. Someone else must have sent it in, but who? Then I recalled that the words were written in my hand-writing.

The person who wrote it could only be me.

It shook me to the core that *I* couldn't recognize my own actions, and that I thought that I was someone else. I had been so busy spinning in so many directions that I was losing control of my thoughts, my identity, perhaps even my sanity. I thought of Johnny Waterman and his invisible friend Pierre, and I saw that no matter what I accomplished, it was an empty victory if I couldn't recall my achievements or lost my sense of self.

Once I realized this, my compulsion to do *everything* drifted away.

Thanks to the generous spirit of my co-workers, we saved those jobs, and I stepped down from the union. I retired my conductor's wand, and didn't win the borough assembly, which was a relief. My life returned to normal as I went back to being a person with one job and a couple of hobbies.

For a long time I wondered about that manic spring, trying to understand why I felt compelled to do so much and stretch myself beyond reason. After years of perspective I realized that those months, from March to May, were the anniversary months of my little daughter's life, from birth to death.

Unable to be her mother, I took on everything else.

31.

❧ The Price of Choice ❧

IN 1986, TOM'S COMPANY SPONSORED a fall retreat to a fishing lodge on the Kenai River. I had fished as a kid on Lake Ontario but this was the first time in Alaska.

Out on the river, I hooked a king salmon that dove under the boat trying to snap the line. My rod was strung with nylon line rated for twenty-five pounds, but this fish felt a lot bigger than that. I moved with it when it jerked, reeling it in slowly so the line didn't snap, allowing the fish to fight itself out without giving it one inch of slack.

Eventually I reeled it up to the side of the boat where the guide held the net. The fish barely fit in it, and it took two men to lift it into the boat. Tom told me how long I had been reeling it in and I thought he was joking. It seemed as if it had been only a few minutes but I had been fighting the crafty old king for three-quarters of an hour. I was glad it hadn't out-smarted me, but it made me feel queasy when our fishing guide bashed it on the head with a chunk of wood and the fish moaned like a scared dog. I will be quite happy never to hear that again.

They hung it on a scale and it stretched down to my knees, weighing in at a hefty seventy-four pounds. My king salmon was the second-biggest fish caught on the river that week. After having it stuffed, I promptly retired from fishing. I had more than enough laurels to rest on with that giant fish on my wall nearly as long as my couch.

As the autumn days grew shorter and crisper, I prepared for another milestone. My black-belt test was set for December. Nine guys would test with me. The master invited every black belt in town to help him test us. He said it was going to be a barbecue because we were going to be "roasted." He was only half-joking.

Tom videotaped the whole thing. The master and his volunteers, including Kit, worked us over starting with drills, almost two dozen forms (katas), and then on to disarming an armed attacker who came at us with a knife (real) and a gun (unloaded). Then came the free fighting, including the master's specialty—street fighting. This was an intense combat style that allowed full contact, multiple attackers, and no rules.

The ordeal continued throughout the day. After six hours, the master declared that our test was over. Battered to exhaustion, the ten of us slumped to the floor. It would be half an hour before any of us were able to stand up.

The master went off to confer with his fellow black belts, commenting before he left that our faces looked "kind of funny." Glancing into a wall mirror, I saw he was right. Drained of blood, our faces were nearly as white as our sweat-drenched uniforms. We *did* look funny in a sick sort of way. But we were too tired to laugh, too tired to talk, too drained to do anything but gasp for breath.

As I looked at the parchment-white faces around me, I knew we didn't need words. I could see the same thought in each pair of eyes. We had not quit. We could have walked out at any time—abandoned the physical abuse and gone off to enjoy a nice meal and a beer. But we refused to give up. The master could deny us the rank, but our will was unbroken. No one could take that from us.

The master returned with a stern face. Behind him, the black belts were grinning because all ten of us passed. This made me the eighth female martial artist in Fairbanks promoted by the master to the rank of black belt. I was about to enter a whole new level in the world of karate.

My work at the state survey was reaching new heights, too. Now I had my own office, no longer parked in someone else's coffee pot corner. Bookshelves lined the walls with my own reference volumes, my own drafting table, and a window with a fine view toward town. No longer grudgingly accepted as a token anything, I was a full-fledged member of this rare breed of geological explorers in a place that had been an elite men's club for so long. I had gotten here by myself with dogged determination. My name was on maps from all parts of the state. I was good on any crew, could work any terrain, and put in savagely long hours on the most mind-numbing chores. On my geochemistry maps, I coordinated hundreds of samples, thousands of analyses, and massaged them all into table-sized sheet maps even a teenager could understand.

Thanks to my teaching, I had become adept at breaking down complex geological issues into plain English that anyone could follow. For this, I became a go-to person. The mayor needed a briefing on interior Alaska's gas potential? Set up a meeting. The National Park Service needed sixty million years of rock history squeezed onto a plaque? Give me a call. I was recognized for what I did and what I could do; there was no stopping me now.

Four days after my black-belt ordeal, the bruises still healing, I stood over my drafting table and laid out the topographic map for a project planned the following summer. It was a mop-up project in the White Mountains, filling in a gap we hadn't quite got to the year before with Dr. Thomas Smith's big crew. This little project wouldn't have helicopters or a big budget, but it was mine, or at least half mine. I would run this project with Dr. Diana Solie, the state survey's other female hard-rock mapper. Diana was an experienced field geologist and would be good company.

As I smoothed the folds of the map, a colleague came into my office, flushed with excitement.

"Is it true?" he said. "Is Nerco leaving the state? The whole company? Are you moving away?"

Tom had worked his way up at Nerco Minerals from his first job running a bulldozer gold-recovery crew, to overseeing the company's computer systems, to a market-analysis job, and then to his current job as head of commodity sales. He would have known if a major move was afoot. There had not been even a whiff of rumor about a corporate move.

"Relax," I said. "It's just a rumor. We're not going anywhere."

I went back to work, planning the best way to hike into the White Mountains.

Then Karen Clautice rushed into my office.

"It's on the radio," she said. "There was an official announcement. Nerco is leaving Alaska. The whole company is moving to Portland, Oregon!"

I picked up the phone and called Tom. Yes, he said, it was true. He had just been told. The entire company was moving to Vancouver, Washington, across the Columbia River from Portland. Nerco would no longer be a big fish in a small pond as it repositioned itself to become a global market leader. The company wanted Tom on board as a vice president. It would be a huge promotion. All he had to do was agree to move with the company. He knew that my job, having just survived the threat of layoffs, wasn't safe and that we couldn't afford to lose his job. Nerco wanted a decision, *are you with us or not?* And he had agreed to go without talking to me.

Tom couldn't talk long because his office was in chaos. That night when he came home, he looked shell-shocked, too exhausted to say much, having spent the day listening to distraught employees, many of them in tears.

Besides, what was there for us to talk about? Tom had said yes. It was a done deal.

Tom's boss, a good guy, called to apologize when he learned that I had heard about the move on the radio. He wanted me to know that Nerco had kept Tom in the dark until the announcement was made. Of course, Tom hadn't known. He already told me that. But his boss's well-intentioned apology didn't do me much good. The fact remained that Tom had been blind-sided and coaxed into making a decision in the heat of the moment without giving him a chance to talk it over with me. I was stuck with it.

Was I angry? Words don't come close to describing how upset I was. Right then, my darling husband didn't seem like much of a prize.

Then Tom came home with the news that Nerco was going to give me a job. This was a generous gesture. On paper, it looked ideal: Tom would get his promotion, and I could continue to work. But it wasn't right. It wasn't what I had trained to do. How could I take a job from someone else knowing I wasn't the first choice, or the second, or the third? How could I accept a position created to keep me quiet? I had not fought my way up the ladder for every inch of respect to end up disrespecting myself.

Tom and I always had given each other so much freedom to chase our careers, even with jobs that forced us to spend large chunks of time apart. We had never discussed this particular what-if question. We hadn't seen this coming. So when it came, and he was asked what he wanted, he told them. He had made his choice. Now it was my turn to make mine. I could either keep Tom or hold onto the life I had worked for so hard.

I couldn't have both.

For me, it was a lose-lose situation, a bitter equation, but there was something else to consider. We had been talking about adopting a child from the same agency that my brother had come from so many years before. It was a complicated process requiring hours of interviews and letters from our employers, our bank, and our friends. If we split up, that little girl with no mommy would never be mine.

Tom wanted her, too. Tom and I understood each other on a deep level. No one had ever understood me the way he did. Right from the start, we both knew that we had something special—that *we* were the real deal. To find this was a blessing. To lose it because of a crush of circumstance would be tragic. Yet, how could I leave Alaska?

The move was set for the following summer, six months away. I had to decide. Move or stay? Every day, as the deadline crept closer, the endless debate raged in my mind. It was an impossible choice.

My life became a continuous migraine. Every evening, I wondered if this would be the last time I would see the flaming sunset above the Alaska Range. With every drive into the Chena Hills, I wondered if I'd ever see anything as stark and bright as that northern view. Every quiet delight brought a shiver of pain.

One morning in late spring, Dr. Smith was waiting for me in my office. Something was wrong.

"We need maps," he said without a hello. "One of our people is missing. His plane is overdue. We need to send crews out to find him."

"Who?" I asked, feeling sick in my gut. Which of my friends was in trouble? What member of my family of explorers might not be coming home?

"John Dillon."

My stomach dropped. As geologists, we all knew the dangers. But Dillon was also a pilot, and that compounded the risks.

We hired every plane and helicopter we could find and sent dozens of volunteer searchers to the Brooks Range. I didn't go. I stayed in town and coordinated efforts from there, keeping the big radio by my side day and night.

It felt strange not to be out with the search crews. But already the mountains were pulling away from me, refusing to tell their secrets to the one who was thinking of leaving, the one with the traitorous heart.

32.

⤳ *Farewell* ⤳

*A*FTER WEEKS OF SEARCHING, the remains of John Dillon's airplane were found. He had crashed into the side of a nameless mountain, one of hundreds in Alaska's northernmost range.

I had met John in a burst of firecrackers. It was hard to accept that in an instant this magnificent life force, this Technicolor personality, had been taken from us forever.

The governor of Alaska delivered the eulogy at John's funeral. Our colleague was buried with honors. A memorial scholarship was created as a lasting tribute. And the stark rugged mountain on which he died was given his name.

As I reflected on John's work, one summer stood out. It was the year that I'd planned to join his crew in the Brooks Range. He was going to try something completely new to arctic exploring—packing into his camp with llamas. Having grown up with horses, I liked the idea. But Dr. Smith talked me out of joining John's expedition because he wanted me to run his geochemical crew.

After we wrapped up that project, I flew a few hundred miles west to a site near the town of Farewell, and worked in a camp for Tom Bundtzen. We were nearly through for the season when a surprise visitor arrived from town. It was Holister Grant, who had recently been promoted. With his new administrative duties, he didn't get out into the field as much as he would have liked. But he was able to clear his schedule for a while to come to Bundtzen's camp, and we were glad to have him.

It was always cause for celebration when someone came out from Fairbanks. It was good to see a new face, especially a friend, and we were hungry to hear the news from civilization.

Visitors usually brought fresh supplies, too. You didn't fly out to a bush camp empty-handed. The back of the chopper would be loaded with fresh produce, a cooler of meat, unspoiled cheese, and a few bottles of liquor.

Holister brought more alcohol than we expected—many cases of beer and several bottles of whiskey. It was his birthday. Not just any birthday; he had turned forty that day. This was more than a celebration; it was a landmark. Conveniently, we had the supplies to celebrate in style.

Someone presented Holister with a gift—a bottle of wine. This simple gesture moved him deeply as he told us this was the only birthday gift he had received. This seemed odd because he had just come from town where he lived with his wife.

We knew Holister's wife was no fan of Fairbanks, and didn't share his passion for rocks. Like most of the spouses, she didn't appreciate that his career took him away every summer, and she didn't go out of her way to socialize with his work friends. In such a small and tight-knit community, her absence was noticeable. I had never met her.

They had moved back to California a few times, but Holister's heart brought them back to Alaska where he connected the histories of the rock units like a giant puzzle. The children they wanted had never come.

Then, miraculously, they had a baby girl, a healthy little thing. She was eighteen months old that summer. Their family was complete at last. So why was Holister spending his special birthday in a tent camp with us?

We broke out the liquor. This was not just a party; it was our *duty* as Holister's friends to do whatever we could to make it a memorable night. There was a banjo twanging, a guitar strumming, and lots of bad singing as we danced around the campfire like the pack of drunken fools that we were after three months in the field. In a single night we drank our way through every drop of liquor.

When Holister finally stumbled away toward his tent, too sick to drink any more, Bundtzen went with him to make sure he didn't pass out on the tundra. We would not be getting an early start the next day, and knew there would be a price for that night.

We didn't yet know the extent of the cost.

Early the next morning, a call came in from town on the big radio hooked up to a car battery in the work tent. One of the guys rushed to get Bundtzen. After taking the call, Bundtzen emerged from the tent, his face as gray as oatmeal. He wouldn't tell us what happened. All he said was that Holister had to get back into town right away.

Holister was in no shape to fly. Even so, they dragged him from his tent and loaded him into the chopper like a piece of broken luggage, sandwiched between Bundtzen and Jeff. The rest of us watched them go. With the helicopter gone, we couldn't get any work done that day. We had a week's worth of ground to cover before we could go back to town to our families and live like real people again with houses and toilets and sinks. But instead, we were stuck in camp wondering what was going on.

Late in the day the story leaked out: Holister's wife was dead. She had committed suicide.

The night of Holister's birthday, his wife had dropped off their toddler with another geologist, supposedly to go to the airport. She had asked him to watch her child for an hour, and of course he agreed.

She didn't go to the airport. She went back home and wrote two letters. One was to Holister; the other was to the geologist watching her child who she knew would come looking for her. The second letter was specific: her body was out back, don't touch anything, call the police. Then she went into the back yard and shot herself with Holister's bear rifle.

Jeff stayed in town with Holister while Bundtzen returned to camp. We finished the work but it was a listless chore, overshadowed by the terrible cloud of Holister's shattered life.

As the crew packed up the camp, I thought about the different ways we dealt with our lives. We spent so much time in a hostile wilderness. And at the end of the day when the sunset was glorious, it was worth all the effort to find myself on a high ridge with wilderness stretching in all directions. Sometimes in the distance I could see where I had been dropped off in the morning and view the entire length of the traverse and all the miles of ground I had just mapped. At those moments, I knew that some part of me was forever linked with those rocks in a way no one else could be. It was such a raw joy to take all that into the lungs, the eyes, the soul.

Yet, to Holister's wife, Alaska wasn't a beautiful thing. The same arctic sun, the smell of summer pollen, and the far-mountain view— they were just accomplices to her suffering. To her, Alaska represented unbearable pain. To me, it wasn't just a place; it was a friend, one of the best friends I would ever have.

We were so different, she and I. She couldn't wait to get away and went to such a terrible length to make it happen. Now I was contemplating leaving myself. If I left, would I ever again feel the primal rush of excitement as I headed out to the field? Would I ever again know that all-embracing rapture of the wilderness and the grateful rediscovery of everyday human comforts and delights upon returning?

Most of all, I wondered if I would ever be happy again.

As I weighed my choices and looked to the future, it took me a while to admit a certain truth. My tight-knit world of Alaskan geological explorers had grown smaller. Looking at pictures from my wedding only eight years before, I counted the eager young faces of friends and colleagues who never would have families of their own. It was a cold shock to realize that nearly one-fifth of them had died. One fell into a glacial crevasse. Another slipped on a boulder and split his head on a rock. And some, like Johnny Waterman the eccentric mountain-climber, simply disappeared. We would never know how they died.

Others, like John Dillon, died in aviation accidents. I would, no doubt, have been among them in that Hatcher Pass helicopter crash except for the slimmest whisper of chance.

And there was Jeff, smiling Jeff, who broke his back before I met him and wore a halo of tragedy that made me fear that his life would be cut short, too. And it was. Jeff was shot in the back in a gun-cleaning accident. This time, his spine didn't heal. He spent two years in lingering pain until pneumonia took what was left.

Nerco moved south in July 1987, exactly ten years after I arrived in Alaska. I stayed behind to work on my follow-up expedition to the White Mountains. I could not leave a project unfinished.

When the field season was over and all those rock samples had been brought back to our warehouse and laid to rest for the winter next to the twisted fragments of Dillon's plane, I would go south, too. I needed this new baby girl with the eager black eyes to be mine.

I would leave more than my job. This would be the end of my exploration career. All the rocks in Washington state had been walked over, picked through, and mapped decades ago.

Goodbye to the "kozy cabin" on Chena Hills that we'd rescued from shameful neglect and turned into a home. Goodbye to the karate classes with Kit and the master and all the people who trained with me and who graciously shared every bit of their strength.

I would see no more winter wonderland whizzing by from the back of a dog sled, or midnight sun, or northern lights. There would be no more organizing conventions, or fighting the union, or conducting the symphony, or being filled with that glorious feeling that I could do anything.

I had been wrong. I couldn't do everything.

I could not stay.

Epilogue

OUR NEW ADOPTED BABY GIRL arrived from Korea in time to be an Alaskan; it says so right there on her foreign-born birth certificate. With her big cheeks and black eyes, she looked the part. We named her after a classic—little baby Yvonne.

My last visit before I left Fairbanks was to the cemetery on the hill with a special section among the birch trees that held so many graves because they were small. Karen promised to drop by once in a while with fresh flowers. I knew I might not ever walk again among the little markers or see the toys next to the headstones, their plastic colors faded by seasons of sun and snow, always there, never removed, as if the wild animals and the wind itself knew not to touch them, these favored toys of a child taken too young and too soon. Of all the goodbyes, this was the hardest of all as I felt I was losing little Tessa all over again.

But my life went on and my motherhood, too. In the Pacific rainforest of Washington state, Tom and I raised two daughters—little Yvonne and Amy, who came from Thailand a few years later. With their arrival, our family felt complete. These girls would grow strong and proud. They would listen as I explained my view of the mysteries of life and hear all the things I never got to tell my first daughter, who had so little time.

Tom's job as the vice president at Nerco proved to be a springboard for his career. After seven years in Washington, we moved back to Alaska, to Juneau this time. And although they say you never can come home again, and Juneau is more than eight hundred miles (1,327 km) from Fairbanks, it still felt every bit like coming home.

After two years in Juneau, we moved to London, England, then Utah, and back to England, every move another rise for Tom up the corporate ladder. He reached such heights that he could hardly go higher. After his decision to leave Fairbanks, sealed in the heat of the moment, he learned to consult the people who matter before making choices that would affect his family.

Yvonne Grace put down roots in Wasilla, where she handles the paperwork for her husband's construction firm. In an area of seismic activity, she uses her training to site their building projects on firm, stable ground.

My sister Stephanie's geological summer in Alaska was put to good use. She went on to become a marine geologist near San Francisco. She is one of the few women to explore the bottom of the ocean in the *Alvin*, the U.S. Geological Survey's pioneering submersible. Carving her own legacy in the scientific world, she is mentioned in the book *Waterbaby: the Story of Alvin*, by Victoria Kaharl.

My older sister Christine settled near the redwood forests of northern California. She turned her home into a one-room school house for her six sons to provide them with a solid foundation for making their own way into the great wide world.

After Ed returned to New York, he graduated from college, ran his own car dealership, and had two fine children. Together Ed and I bought a little piece of land on the shore of Lake Ontario where we can take our families camping, with a store right down the road.

My father never retired to the west, but contented himself with visits to his daughters, providing him with ample adventures. Looking back, I think that was his plan all along—to have his son nearby to help build things on the farm and to have his daughters blazing distant trails to satisfy his traveling spirit.

As for me, I have experienced many lives that I would have missed had I remained in Fairbanks. For seven years in Washington state, I ran my own karate dojo and a miniature horse farm. From my ranch house, with its view of the volcano-flattened Mount Saint Helens, I wrote a book on Romanian adoption and worked as an adoption coordinator for the same agency that brought my daughters home.

In Juneau, I reconnected with old friends, made jewelry from dinosaur teeth, and taught writing at the University of Alaska Southeast on the most exquisite campus imaginable—a cedar cathedral of learning that backed onto a glacial-fed lake.

In England, I earned a PhD and traveled around Europe. Then it was back to the states to live in the Wasatch Mountains of Utah where my daughters and I could ride our horses from the barn straight up into the hills. In the historic mining town of Park City, I wrote film reviews for a local newspaper and hosted my own morning radio show.

Returning to England once again, the world opened up in new directions. I entered my artwork in international competitions, taught art at a hospice, and worked on some films.

In all my reincarnations, the one thing that I return to again and again is the magic of writing. It is the most personal, yet the most exposing of arts, both painfully private and outrageously public at the same time. I am constantly amazed where I find inspiration and where it finds me. I am awed by the way writing holds the collective text of humanity, defining who we are and what we are as a species. Yet, at the same time, it defines each one as unique, yielding a fingerprint of the soul and explaining why each of us matters.

Both product and process, this rich harvest of contradictions, this most paradoxical of arts has become for me another Alaska, a place where impossible things can happen, where once again I can be anything and do anything on the strength of my words.

Every once in a while, I still get the odd question about my igneous rocks in the Alaska Range, and it surprises me that I remain the authority, that no one has re-examined those rocks. Even stranger is that the answer comes readily. *Yes, the feldspar in the Sugar Loaf rhyolite has a high calcium content.* I might forget where I just laid down my keys but the details of Sugar Loaf's plagioclase ratios are permanently hard-wired into my head.

In May 2010, I returned to Fairbanks for a special occasion. Tom was asked to give the commencement speech at the University of Alaska Fairbanks that year and to accept an honorary doctorate degree. It was a grand moment to see Tom, one of the university's most successful graduates, recognized for his achievements in the mining world.

As I prepared for the trip back, I was reminded of my first flight to Fairbanks thirty-three years before and of the couple from Ohio who were returning for their alumni reunion, so eager to see old friends, so excited to return to a place where they were not born, a place where they no longer lived, but a place that would always be home. I didn't understand it back then, but it became clear as the wheel came full circle.

After Tom received his award, we threw a celebration party in a log hotel on the banks of the Chena River. Karl Hanneman stood up to propose the first toast, just as he had at our wedding. Beside me was Yvonne Grace; Tom's mother, Rosemarie; Carol and Vaughn Hoeffler; Dr. Smith and his wife Judy; Steve and Karen Clautice; Bruce Campbell and his family; Nancy Hanneman; and Dr. Tripp and his wife Julia. All had come to our wedding in a room with log walls, very much like this one, and were back with us once more, along with other old friends we had known through the years, people like Shirley, Diana and Dan Solie; Roger Burgraff; Paul Metz; and Fran and Tom Bundtzen, to celebrate another festive occasion. Despite some silvering of hair, I swear that no one looked a day older. What I saw were the smiling faces, the proud faces of Alaska, which remain with me wherever I am.

I wonder sometimes if her heart hadn't given out, what kind of person my Tessa would have been. What would have fueled her passion? Where might she have looked for her dreams? I wonder if her spirit will stay a child forever, or be reborn to someone else. Perhaps I will find out at the end of the trail.

For now, each morning brings fresh colors to the dawn in shades that call to me and whisper impossible dreams. And I, having lived in that wild sweet corner on the top of the world, find there is still enough of that wide-eyed girl, so ready to charge through the tundra, so unwilling to give up, to listen.

Acknowledgments

$\mathcal{T}$HESE STORIES ARE ALL TRUE, or as true as I remember them. In some cases, I have changed the names of individuals, but the incidents and conversations are as I recall them. Others might remember things differently. If you do, please get in touch. The next time I'm in town, we can swap stories at the Howling Dog or another drinking establishment of your choice.

It has been a treasured honor to have been a part of my Alaskan "family," my friends, colleagues, and mentors with their quirks and foibles and hearts as big as the great wide north. This book is a tribute to their spirit, sometimes stubborn, sometimes outrageous, but always unforgettable.

Big thanks go to Lael Morgan who believed in the project enough to make me rewrite it again and again until I got it right.

I would like to acknowledge Lisa Hagan, who believed in an early draft when no one else would look, and to my advance readers, Sue Bohane, Patti Boone, Mandy Griffith, and Shirley Huang, who provided encouragement and advice.

Thanks to my family, to my parents who encouraged me to follow my dreams, to my grandfather who showed me the heart and soul of a writer, and to my siblings who were there for it all. Huge thanks to Tom, who has supported all my efforts, no matter how crazy they seemed, and to our daughters, Yvonne and Amy, who are off chasing their own dreams.

Thanks to Allen Price, general bridge and building supervisor of the Alaska Railroad Corporation for providing statistics on the Ferry bridge. It is worth mentioning that since visiting Ferry, the Alaska Railroad Corporation has provided a walkway along the west side of the Ferry bridge. While it does not encourage public use of the walkway, it does tolerate public usage and will not cite trespass for use of the walkway. However, the railroad is adamant that unauthorized persons must not occupy any other portion of the bridge. I could not agree more.

Finally, a monster thanks to my writer's group: Meg Gardiner, Adrienne Dines, Kelly Gerrard, Nancy Fraser, Suzanne Davidovac, Tammye Huf, Kathy Montgomery, Sue Graunke, David Wolfe, Hee Jung Westcoat, Jennifer Spears, Betsy Speer, and all the rest who generously pooled their formidable talents over the years to be my sounding board.

Index

Readers' Group Questions

1. The author's life was changed by a chance remark (the education professor's unfulfilled longing to go to the Brooks Range). Have you ever had a chance remark or small incident change the course of your life?

2. The author speaks of a destiny that drew her north. Do you believe life is governed by destiny or a series of events/accidents (or both)?

3. The book presents an unusual premise: "if at first you don't succeed, try something that's harder." This strategy seems to have worked for the author. Do you think there might be a reason this counter-intuitive strategy might work or do you feel the author's success with this rationale was merely a string of luck?

4. Many of the people the author met in Alaska had strong personalities. Why might this be so?

5. Has this book changed the way you think about how scientific or geographic knowledge is advanced?

6. The book discusses land lotteries of the west, where a state would offer the winners the opportunity to purchase the land at market value. This was a common means to distribute and settle unpopulated regions. Do you feel this was a successful way to encourage a state's growth and prosperity? If not, what might you recommend?

7. What lessons (either by positive example or pitfalls to avoid) might this book provide for a person choosing their educational or career path?

8. What lessons (either by positive example or pitfalls to avoid) might this book provide for a person dealing with issues involving loss?

9. The author discusses her view that karate, a highly physical sport, requires a mental component to succeed. Do you feel this might be

a metaphor for how one might deal with his/her life? How much of a person's success do you believe is shaped by their mental outlook?

10. If you were to live in the wilderness for five days with only what you could carry (including food), what would you bring? How might you trim your gear and supplies down to make it manageable for carrying? Write down your packing list and discuss.

11. The author touches briefly on the importance of the bond between a dog musher and their lead dog, which in extreme survival conditions, can mean the difference between life and death. Have you ever experienced a heroic event by an animal or a pet that made a significant contribution to your safety or life?

13. The author chose to leave Alaska for the sake of her family. Discuss.

About the Author

ℬORN IN UPSTATE NEW YORK, Mary Albanese attended the State University of New York at Stony Brook on Long Island before arriving in Alaska. She earned her master's degree in geoscience at the University of Alaska Fairbanks, and spent ten years there as a geological explorer.

After leaving Fairbanks, she moved to the Pacific Northwest and ran a karate studio and a miniature horse farm. She also served as an international adoption counselor and wrote for various adoption organizations.

Returning to Alaska, she worked as a writing instructor at the University of Alaska Southeast in Juneau. Later, she lived in the Wasatch Mountains of Utah, where she hosted a weekend morning radio show on Park City's KPCW. She went on to earn her PhD in writing education at the University of Reading in England.

The author has won numerous awards for her writing in a wide range of genres, and has had one of her short films screened at Cannes Film Festival. Her artwork, a constant companion throughout the years, has been displayed in international exhibitions. She lives with her husband Tom in the English countryside and continues to write on a diverse range of subjects, from fiction to non-fiction, and television and film projects.

Reading Recommendations

FOR THOSE WHO ENJOY WOMEN'S MEMOIRS

Accidental Adventurer
The Story of the First Woman to Climb Mt. McKinley
Barbara Washburn with Lew Freedman, paperback, $14.95

Cold River Spirits
Whispers from a Family's Forgotten Past
Jan Harper-Haines, paperback, $14.95

Kay Fanning's Alaska Story
Memoir of a Pulitzer Prize-Winning Newspaper Publisher
Kay Fanning, paperback, $17.95

Raising Ourselves
A Gwitch'in Coming of Age Story from the Yukon River
Velma Wallis, paperback, $15.95

Sisters
Coming of Age & Living Dangerously
Samme & Aileen Gallaher, paperback, $14.95

Surviving the Island of Grace
A Life on the Wild Edge of America
Leslie Leyland Fields, paperback, $17.95

These titles can be found or special-ordered from your local bookstore,
or they may be ordered 24 hours a day at 800-950-6663.
More Epicenter titles, including many personal stories,
may be found at www.EpicenterPress.com.

ALASKA BOOK ADVENTURES™
Epicenter Press, Inc.
www.EpicenterPress.com